Got Your Affairs in Order?

Catharina Bowers

Copyright © 2021 by Catharina Bowers

All rights reserved.
ISBN: 9798564171410

Dedication

I dedicate this book to
Piet and Laura Spaans,
my wonderful parents,
I owe them so much!
They taught me to never give up
and stay positive,
and I did.
I knew that someday my prince
would come, and he did in the form
of a king, Lorne King.

Love, *Cat*

Contents

Dedication 3

-Preface- 7

Acknowledgements 13

Coulda, Woulda, Shoulda! 17

Let's talk about it! 27

80's wasn't my best decade 33

The dreaded week in 86 43

Mom's Funeral 53

August 1995 59

9/11 2001 70

Piet – October 2002 75

SARS 91

Viola –September 2007 99

Time for a new hip or two 104

In Michael's Own Words 111

Mitral Valve 115

Decompression Surgery	130
Bill - August 2018	137
I Visit the Sick	144
Do They Help?	151
Pandemic's	145
It Keeps Coming	164
Thank You Charlotte	190
It's ok to be angry.	197
Run for the hills	215
Live In Peace	219
Where Do I Start?	227
Got Your Affairs in Order?	248
Is the Cost Stopping You?	254
MAID	257
After the Funeral	263
Losing a Child	268

Appendix 1 274

Appendix 2 276

Appendix 3 277

Appendix 4 288

About the Author Rev. Catharina Bowers 290

Contributing Author Rev. Michael Bishop 292

-Preface-

Some things you really need to talk about!

Nobody wants to talk about dying, it is as if you are going to talk about it, and then it's going to happen a day sooner. But sooner or later you have to talk about it. Actually, you really should talk to someone in your family about it. You are not jinxing the time line to have it happen any sooner than it will actually happen.

I remember in the late 70's I sold Crown Life insurance to people, to anyone who would listen. And of course that included family and friends and complete strangers. At some point in the presentation you discussed how long they planned to live, you took down their health history, their financial history, in some cases they needed to have a health exam or a physical to determine if they could be insured or would there be additional premiums because of health issues like diabetes, cancer, and asthma for example.

I actually had people cancel a few appointments because they didn't want to talk about death...oddly enough, they too did pass, but their family would have been a little better off if they had taken the time to talk to me. My goodness that was more than 40 years ago; time flies!

In a CTV news report in January of 2018, it was found that according to a new poll, 51 per cent of Canadians did not have a will.

"A significant number say the reason they haven't written a will is that they're 'too young' to worry about it (25%)," a written statement by the Angus Reid Institute, which conducted the poll, said. "And almost as many say they don't have enough assets to make a will worthwhile (23%)."

According to the poll, another eight per cent said that the main reason they don't have a will is that they "don't want to think about dying."

And in my own personal experience; that was about true, half the home owners I spoke to didn't have a will.

In the USA during the same time frame, the total number of people with Wills was only 41%. And probably the same reasons exist.

Sometimes it was the cost of making a lawyers appointment that prevented a Last Will and Testament from being written. If you go to the appendix at the back of the book you will find some websites, where you can actually find Will and Power of Attorneys on line.

When you are young, you don't think of dying or being permanently impaired with an illness or from an accident. And when you think about it, I am sure you will be able to think of someone you went to school with that was in a terrible accident, and was laid up for quite some time, having bones set, legs set and learning how to walk again.

Well I did believe that *'it won't happen to me.'* But the thing is; it did. Accidents, illness and death does not discriminate. It doesn't care if you are a good person or a bad person, doesn't care about the colour of your skin, it couldn't care less if you are rich or poor, educated or no education, whether you have a wife, or kids...whether you are happy or sad...it doesn't think nor doesn't it come into play. If you are going to be struck by lightning...it will hit you. If it is your time and you are in a car, or on a sidewalk ready to cross the street...it will happen!

I am not a person, who thinks the worst of everything, I am actually quite positive. I just believe you will die when you are meant to die and not a minute sooner.

As I write this, I am 72 years old. I have been in a few situations where I honestly thought, ok, today's the day. I woke up after having a bilateral mastectomy in May of 1982 I thought it was early morning, the day after my surgery. I was bandaged from my ribcage to my neck and I had little hoses coming out with little round accordions attached and it was draining blood and fluid away from the surgery sites. The windows were open the curtains were billowing, and I heard the Lord's Prayer being recited. I thought, I must be in heaven, because it was so bright and light and white. I was drugged and woozy within a few minutes I realized I was still here on the planet I was laying in a bed in the hospital. It wasn't a near death experience; I just thought I had died.

But for the grace of God go I...It wouldn't be the first time that someone (young in 1982 I was only 34) for some reason dies while on the operating table or has a blood clot that travels to their brain. Did I have my shit together? No I didn't.

It made me think. That if you own something, a car, house, stocks or jewelry, have children, you need to be prepared. Whether you are young or middle age or elderly, you need to be prepared. You need to have your paper work in order.

Acknowledgements

I am so grateful to still be alive. I thank God every day that I am still here. To my husband Lorne King; who has stood by me through some very tough times with my health. Thank you darling for loving me unconditionally, and for always being there for me. You continue to be my rock and best friend. I'll love you forever!

I also wish to thank our friend Paul, my former family physician Dr. Laroche for his skilled care, knowledge, and quick assessment. Your diagnosis was right on point. I continue to get excellent health care from my new family physician Dr. Mara Hollingsworth, you get things done! I thank you. To Dr. Akshay Bagai my interventional cardiologist, Dr. Michael Gofeld, my pain specialist and Dr. Kevin Koo, my orthopedic spinal surgeon, I thank you all for keeping me mobile and ticking.

My sons Kurt and Peter Hansen and your families thank you. I learn so much from you. My precious grandchildren, Robyn, Lauren, Haylee, Nicholas and Kelsi you mean the world to me, I love you and I am so proud of each of you. COVID you rascal, I don't see my children often enough!

When I first thought about writing this book, I had a much spicier title in mind, and I thought, 'Better tone it down,' I wouldn't want to offend anyone. So I ran the idea past a few trusted friends. Shirley J. Mein, author, friend and financial advisor, who recognized how many people were not adequately prepared in case of a lingering illness or a sudden death. I appreciate your friendship, advice and your encouragement.

Thank you to my delightful friend Susie Baird; who was willing to let me share some stories and insights regarding her late husband Douggie 'Wesley' Baird. Your encouragement, advice and friendship throughout the years and this project are so appreciated. You are special to me.

Our good friend Rev. Michael Bishop also thought this book was a worthy project. Michael is a cherished father and grandfather, with serious health issues. He feels we all need to be prepared for the future. His background in ministry and hospital chaplaincy proved invaluable. Thank you so much Michael, my brother.

My sweet girlfriend Lynda Liscio and her husband Erik have stood by me through many of the adventures I have written about, I value your friendship and your counsel. You have never steered me wrong. I also value you as my sister; you are like family to me, and I love you!

Jackie Detoro, my sister in law, but actually more of a little sister, I have been thoroughly blessed with you and your family in my life. You are precious.

My cousin Mia Spaans, my Dutch sister who drops everything to visit her Canadian sister when I have needed her. Her courage and strength and spontaneity continues to be appreciated by me.

Thank you Mia, you mean the world to me, as does neighbour and friend Yvonne Burgess, who is a like minded spiritual woman, who keeps me grounded literally, and will come out to play when I need to make a snow angel.

Thank you all my family and friends! I know I am blessed with some very special people in my life. I unfortunately can't name you all, but please know that you have certainly contributed to me, the woman who had much to learn, and in some cases endure. But, I am so pleased that you are all part of my blessed life.

To my new friends in Magnetawan, at Trinity United Church, I know it has only been a short time; this darn COVID has thrown a monkey wrench into so much for this community. Thank you, and God Bless you all. *Catharina*

Chapter 1:

Coulda, Woulda, Shoulda!
If only things had been done differently by my parents or by me... Have you ever thought, if only I had made a different decision...a different choice? Yes, if only!

I wouldn't have married the 3 husbands that I had over the past 50 years. And learned the lessons I did. And put up with the stories I did. How boring my life would have been.

We were watching something on TV at the hotel last week when I went for my pain treatment. It showed a promo for a series out of Australia, and I said, "You know if my parents had a choice to make back in 1953 when they decided to come to Canada." Can you imagine how my life would have been different had my parents immigrated to Australia or South Africa?"

I never would have met Lorne…I wouldn't have had maybe my two boys because I wouldn't have met their dad…I would not have met my sister in law Jackie….had my 3 beautiful nieces…cause my brother's life would have been different too.

OMG…everything would be different in my life. I might have been speaking Afrikaans, or English with an Aussie accent.

My parents would have been the same. But my education could have been different. I could have been a hairdresser, or an actress or a stand-up comic. Who knows? I could have been my own cardiologist, or maybe my heart wouldn't have had a problem. I might have been a teacher, or a nurse or a famous author.

I might have been married to a crocodile wrangler or a cattle rancher, or 'Quigley Down Under' if I had moved to Australia...I could have met Tom Selleck on one of his trips down there 'to find his way down under.'

I instead married a handsome Dane who showed me that he could look after me like the trophy wife he had wanted in a wife who was 18 years younger. He gave me two beautiful sons, Kurt and Peter. And they grew up to be handsome men with terrific families of their own. The outcome with their dad was short lived when he showed more interest in doing his own thing, and not being responsible to look after both his sons. He ripped them out of my arms and heart, no wonder my heart was breaking...a heart can only take so much.

I have been told I am compassionate, positive, calm and a motivational influence to many. How did that happen? It is a choice I tell you. I had a choice to make myself happy. Do I want to be right? Or do I want to be happy? I will always choose happiness. And then when happiness isn't quite enough, there is another choice...chose to live a joyful life.

A life filled with happiness, laughter, and true love and even sacrifice. What is the difference between joy and happy? According to Google's definition is because **happiness** is an emotion in which we "experience feelings ranging from contentment and satisfaction to bliss and intense pleasure," whereas **joy** "is a stronger, less common feeling than **happiness**." We experience **joy** when we achieve selflessness to the point of personal sacrifice.

Had my life been different as I have outlined above...I would probably not be the woman I am today. But I don't think so, because I do need people in my life. I also need the sound of another's voice, the sound of music and the voice of a beautiful singer. Yet I live a fairly quiet life out in the country...but I do like the sound of a joyful noise. Like those woodpecker's on the telephone pole outside or the sound of 'I'm all out of love' on the CD by that lovely group, Air Supply I like to sing along with.

I could have been a miserable old recluse, lives on the edge of town, and peers through the shuttered windows at everyone who passes. Although I don't think so!

Do we ever really know how our life would be different if an alternative choice had been made? I have learned that my lot in life is really very good. And the people in my life are just excellent. I still would have had my cousins, my lovely cousins Paul and Mia Spaans, who are also cousins to each other as well, and few more Paul, Jan, Leo and Ruud who to this day still keep in contact. So everything from my early childhood to the age of 5 would remain status quo. The rest...who knows?

I would never have met my best girlfriend Lynda through her older brother Don. Nor lived in Lindsay with my friend Trish, written lyrics for her music or learned to loosen up and not take life so seriously. I never would have owned horses named Flirt, or Countess Moonbeam; I never would have had the joy of brushing them, cleaning their hooves and riding them through the Purple Woods south of Port Perry. I would never have met Eldon, who taught me self acceptance, or had the joy in seeing my favourite singer Lionel Ritchie or that sexy group that Simon Cowell put together... Il Divo, yes I absolutely love them. I never would have met Arlene Gray, my vocal coach or the group of women singers from

Peterborough, called the Jubilaires, I loved singing with you. Oh, it was the joy of my very short singing career! I would never have met my good friend Michael, or become a hospital chaplain or become a minister.

I would never have moved to Dunchurch with Lorne the love of my life...I wouldn't have my 4 gorgeous granddaughters and my handsome grandson Nick... Lorne would have continued to be a dream that never came true...what a sad state of affairs my life would have been. And I never would have had Wayne as a great brother in law. I would not have known what I had missed!

I could be off living a life of luxury off in some castle or some swanky millionaire's home, being this wonderful creature, but no one to share my joy with.

Or I could be a Dutch lady with a husband named Heinrick who had never been to

Canada to see the Niagara Falls or the little hamlet of Maple Island with its foxes, deer, moose and turkeys.

I would have missed so much just because my parents didn't come to Canada. My entire life would have been different. I would never have twirled a baton as a majorette in the Brooklin parade. I would never have slide down that big pipe (the fire escape) that came out of the 2nd floor of the senior public school in Brooklin, would never have enjoyed the best Halloween ever in that little town back in 1959.

I would not have had Susie and Douggie for friends that in itself would have been a huge loss to me. For not to have had those phone calls, in which Douggie would announce, 'I just called to say I love you.' And God Bless his beautiful wife for being so supportive... by not calling me later to blast me because her husband had chosen to be kind to this elderly minister. I couldn't have missed that for the world. Oh my, I wouldn't have met my friend Shirley, who always keeps things light and full of good laughs, and she after all helped me get my s#*t together! What about Michele and her love of fishing? We never would have gone swimming in our shorts and t-shirts in Labrash Lake that hot, hot day just for shits and giggles, and you know I haven't been swimming since. I'll go this coming year, July 25th for Christmas in July.

I did have the most awesome parents in Piet and Laura, and no matter where we would have ended up, I would have become a happy woman. Never mind the circumstances. I do believe that having been born into this body, there would have been this soul attached to it. And I do believe I would have made the best I could have with this soul and this body, just as I am doing now.

Tomorrow when I see my cardiologist, I will find out a little more about what I need to know about my ever growing calcium around my valve...and see what lies ahead. Whatever I find out, I will not squander my time or life, because I do have Christmas in July to look forward too, and so much more.

So never mind this coulda, woulda, shoulda, it's all immaterial! And it's all irrelevant. Life is what it is, and you make it or leave it the way you want to. All I know is that it's up to me to be the happiest person I can be. It's all in the choices. So what do you choose to do about your own life?

Choose happiness or wealth? Choose health or a fat bank account? I know what I would choose... I have it already, the love of a good man and choose good health, then you are the richest person in your neck of the woods, and isn't that all you can possibly want? I ask you! Because money can't buy you health! Just ask Steve Jobs.

Chapter 2:

Let's talk about it!

The thing is if you decide not to talk about it, your final days could be compromised and full of anxiety and pain. This can all be avoided with a few tough questions for you and your family to answer together.

By talking about your final departure to heaven or wherever you believe you are going to go...and how your final days on earth are going to be spent could speak volumes for some. And why would you leave that to chance...If you are sick in your final months or weeks. Talking about it

before it even happens is a bonus for you. It has opened up the dialogue so that when the time comes, we aren't sitting with the nerves, about how to bring it up for discussion. You have already addressed it before and now it's a matter of doing the paperwork while you are still in a good frame of mind. It is for most people who are aging and preparing for the inevitable a relief to have made these plans and to have talked with their children about not being afraid to talk about it. Share your thoughts and talk about what the others in the family think. Make the decisions together.

From actual experience I can relate what should be done to make it easier for the family to talk and plan a meaningful Celebration of Life.

We all deserve to be honoured and celebrated. There is nothing like a good funeral. And I have been to a few that when you walked away you would think, wow, when I die, I want Rev. Michael Bishop to do my funeral or celebration of life. The way he spoke to those gathered. His ease in dealing with family who were of course grieving, the ease and the lovely way he related to the guests, and included them.

He was a 'real' comfort to those who were there and he made them feel that they were included. Family and friends would come away and say, now, that was a celebration of life. I learned things about the deceased, and by taking the time to interview the family ahead of time, these pearls of wisdom would come out, or a good storey about their youth.

Learning to do a good funeral comes with experience. It's like doing a good wedding. You can only do better if you enjoy doing it and if you are given the opportunity to do something a little different and your client allows you to do it. I do believe that there are people/ministers called to celebrate the lives of our loved one.

A funeral in general is a very emotional time for the family and the guests that you are expecting for the afternoon's service. What the minister says, more or less sets the tone of the event.

I always tell people preplan your funeral or celebration of life. First of all you then have total control over it and how it is going to go. For those who like to plan and know what's going on, this is the way to do it. First of all the funeral is being paid in today dollars as opposed to the future value of the money, and it is very rare that the cost of a funeral will go down. I have never heard of that happening. So that is then the first advantage. The second, you get to select what you want as far as content and how it is going to look, sound and feel. Third the content...you get to supply stories. You decide whether or not you get cremated or buried. You get to pick out the stationary for the cards and guest/condolence book. You decide the charity that people can donate to instead of flowers.

You get to pick out the music. Hymns or Easy Listening music, Uncle John who plays the guitar could do a few numbers or Aunt Helen who plays piano could entertain. Now a days, anything goes. The Church choir could sing. Or you leave a list of your favourite CD's.

Do you want to show a video of your favourite picture of you with your family and friends? Pictures of your wedding, your graduation from university etc. Show picture of your pets, your favourite car, your boat and airplane.

- Do you want someone to read the eulogy?

Are you worried about speaking at mom or dad's service? Do you want to leave a message that could be read by someone else? I've never known a minister to turn down reading a letter by a family member at a celebration of life or a funeral. Don't forget to select pallbearers.

Chapter 3:

80's wasn't my best decade

My parents didn't like or trust my husband. He was not the sensitive, loving man that he had led me to believe he was. He enjoyed his beer more than most things and when he'd had too much, things often got out of hand.

In 1981, I found a nice job at Scarboro Television as a Live TV Producer/Director. I loved that job. Every day I was happy to get up and go to work. I'd get up around 6, get ready, eat a little something and head out the door around 7:45 drive to the studio in Scarborough.

In the morning I would do the behind the scene work, the planning, the lineups, any editing that needed to be done, telephone interviews and setting up shows, arrange for hosts, or go to the hairdresser to get my hair done for the Lifestyle Show etc. I'd run my butt off from 1 to 4PM schlepping backdrops from Monday to Friday the back room area to Studio B. Half hour programs, one hour programs and longer shows that I bit my teeth on, but it was so much fun. I had met wonderful volunteers, people that would show up every week to do their thing and perform their way through their time slot.

My Mom and Dad had a nice life together, they enjoyed traveling to Europe, and back to the Netherlands, Florida, the Bahamas, in the summer time they liked to go north and travel through Ontario, they loved to go to Long Island and visit their friends Janet and Larry in Levittown.

My parents were approaching retirement, and they had planned to travel together, spend time together and enjoy the golden years together. Isn't that what most people work towards? My parents were no different.

In 1983 my mother had been quite ill. After many months of illness she subsequently had surgery at Ajax Pickering General Hospital. At the conclusion of hiatus hernia surgery she was taken to intensive care. The surgeon had spoken to me after her surgery and had said, don't be alarmed, we have taken your mom to Intensive Care, she is bright yellow, she will be in ICU until her normal colour returns.

Apparently when the Dr. Salmon opened her up he saw a tumour on her liver. So this was something that hadn't been counted on when they were planning the surgery. The tumour was sent away for testing, but I was never told the results...I think my Mom wanted to keep it quiet and not alarm us. It was curious however that a number of times she was hospitalized with pneumonia. Each time they withdrew the fluid from her lungs, it was tested. And each time, there were malignant cells found in the fluid. But I don't remember this being discussed in my presence. I never heard the 'C' word, or radiation or chemotherapy mentioned.

Back in the early '80's were things so different? I know we didn't have access to the imaging tests they have today. When people had surgery, often the surgeon went in to do exploratory surgery...dealing with what they had to deal with. All the scans and MRI's that we have at our disposal were not available in the early 80's to everyone. I don't remember Mom going for an MRI or Scan of some kind. It is possible I don't remember. People were also more private.

She may have noticed that having a glass of wine or a rum and coke wouldn't have sat so well in her stomach. Or she may not have wanted a drink with alcohol in it, and that was true. Often Mom would have a little drink with Dad while she was making dinner, and for some reason she had noticed that it didn't taste good any more, or more often lately she wasn't having a drink. Neither my mother nor fathers were big drinkers.

At the time that mom had been so sick; I was working at Scarboro Television in their programming department in Scarborough on Progress Avenue. I had taken a day off here and there to spend with Mom, and to take her shopping at Christmas.

When Mom had left the hospital after her recovery from the hiatus hernia surgery, she really didn't feel so good. She had terrible pain in her shoulders, neck and chest, and nobody was able to figure out what was wrong with my mother. She was back and forth to the surgeon and her family doctor and neither one was able to come up with a solution for Mom.

Mom had always had a business mind. She could figure things out quickly, she did Dad's books and got everything ready for the accountant. She was able to do math in her head, she didn't always need a calculator.

We also noticed that Mom was not able to figure things out as quickly as she had been able to earlier. She was always able to do math very easily and she always did Dad's books from his Texaco service station at Pickering Beach Road and Bayly Ave in Ajax and later on she did it for his repair shop on Finley Ave.

Mom was not doing well. She occasionally became confused and defensive, and quite outspoken about some things. One day she said that she wanted to make Chili Con Carne. She asked Dad to go to the store to buy 'dark red' kidney beans. He came home with kidney beans that didn't say dark red. She was adamant you couldn't make chili with these beans, they weren't dark red. And she wouldn't use them...She didn't make chili until he bought the right ones. Little things like that, we noticed Mom was different, but couldn't figure it out what was wrong.

This one morning I stopped by Mom and Dad's place for coffee before I headed into the city to go to work. This particular morning Mom was confused about Dad's pay stub. Mom had always been sharp as a tack, but that morning, she couldn't figure something out, it was like a brain fog. She was looking at Dad's pay stub that was attached to Dad's pay cheque. She was having a hard time figuring out his banked time and his vacation pay. So when I think about her brain fog and her pain for the prolonged period of time I am quite certain that by today's standard she would have fit the bill for fibromyalgia.

Her terrible pain continued, and still 2 and a half years later, wearing clothes that touched her shoulders, was so painful, she couldn't stand it. My Dad would walk into the room and she could feel movement in the air, and she would complain about the pain in her neck and shoulders.

During surgery patients are moved around and repositioned like a rag doll, and I know this happened with Mom. But we didn't understand the pain she was in, and she couldn't get any relief or a break from it.

Mom too had aggressive behavior to deal with from my brother; so that in combination with the physical pain she had I am convinced she too had had Fibromyalgia. Back in those days, doctors didn't really think about Fibromyalgia too much; since many considered that Fibro didn't really exist. But we now know different. Fibro is now considered to be a neurological disease as opposed to an arthritic or rheumatic disease.

My mother suffered so much. And after a number of years she thought she was doing better. There was still pneumonia to deal with and long stays in the hospital.

Her last Christmas in 1985 was spent in the hospital. They didn't want to let her out for even the day. So we packed up a Christmas dinner for her and visited at dinner time.

When mom came home, she seemed better than she had been in quite some time.

Dealing with chronic illness can be hard on the family but not as hard as it was for her. I used to feel so bad for her, and I couldn't do anything for her to improve how she felt. Mom had to put up with the pain and discomfort. Sometimes you just don't know what to do to make a situation better.

Nowadays people have learned a lot about chronic illness and with the advent of many charitable organization, we are able to learn so much more about different chronic illnesses. What causes them, what they can do help patients. People are also so much more open. We will speak with our family and friends about what is ailing us. So indeed we are more open about illness, and are willing to speak to others about it. And with all the publicity that happens with for the charity walk; for instance the Terry Fox walk for Cancer, the ALS walk, the information that is also dispensed to the public is phenomenal!

Chapter 4:

The dreaded week in 86

Because of circumstances in my personal life I am spending some time with my parents. I had been there about 2 and a half weeks, when one Monday in March, Mom was exceptional well that day; my parents went to visit Ann and Geoff Hooper after dinner. I had gone to the library to do some research for three TV shows I was doing the following day. They had a lovely visit with their friends.

Mom and Dad were not home late, they were back by probably 9 or 9:30PM; Dad had to still work the following day. When they came home, Mom suggested we have some tea. I put the kettle on and made a pot of tea. Dad had gone to bed, mom and I sat on the couch and had tea and ate a few Dutch cookies. It was nice.

At 10:45 I said, "I could sit and talk all night long Mom, but at some time I need to get some sleep, I must go to bed. My mother hugged me that night, as if she knew or felt something different. But we each went off to go to bed. Early in the morning, I was extra quiet. I didn't want to wake her. Her bedroom door was open, I looked into her room and she was fast asleep. She looked so peaceful. I closed the door a bit.

At 8 am I was out the door and when I got to the studio I went to the hairdressers to get my hair done for the 3 shows I was hosting that day. By 10 am I was back at the studio and I was met at the door by Sandy Heal our secretary. She followed me all the way back to my office. She said you need to call home and speak to Jackie. I said ok. What's wrong? Sandy gestured, she didn't know.

I called home, and I spoke to Jackie, and Jackie said, "Cath, Please Come Home!" "I can't, I have 3 shows to do." I heard myself saying to my sister in law. Then I heard Sandy saying that she had looked after it. You go.

"Ok Jack, I'll be there soon, I'm leaving right now." At that moment, I had no idea what was going on. I had never in all these years been asked to come home. So I didn't question it. She wasn't about to tell me anyways.

I was driving along the 401 going eastbound from Scarborough to Ajax, and when I got to the Lawson Road exit, my gut told me what was wrong. I knew my mother was gone. With tears streaming down my face, I got out the tissues and continued home.

Jackie met me at the door with little Sarah…Mom was gone. What a horrible sensation in my head to know you would not speak again with your Mother. I remembered the hug from last night, where she clung on to me so tight and didn't want let go. As if she knew it was the last hug.

My Dad arrived home shortly afterwards and we were all incredulous. We cried.

When Jackie had heard the phone ring that morning and no one answered she went upstairs to see if everything was ok. She thought it strange that no one was answering the phone. And it was.

She then called my brother Pete, Dad and me. Jackie and Pete called 911 and within minutes the police, fire and ambulance arrived. Mom was gone, the ambulance took her to Ajax Hospital and we called the doctor, who told us that because Mom had died at home there would be an autopsy to determine the cause of her death.

That Tuesday afternoon I went to MacEachnies Funeral Home to make some arrangements. I sat in the big office waiting for Mr. MacEachnie to arrive. When he did, he expressed his condolences and asked a few questions about my Mother.

We needed to write an obituary. So we started. He said, "Laura died peacefully in the Ajax Pickering Hospital with her family present." I said NO...He continued... we should put...because, but I wasn't listening. I said no! "My mother died peacefully at home unexpectedly in her sleep. We don't tell a lie to make everyone else feel better! I was sound asleep and so was everyone else. Oh ok, he said. We just got through that awkward dialogue, when suddenly he nodded off; he was out like a light, with his head falling on the desk. I thought he had dropped dead at his desk. It was quite unnerving actually.

I sat and waited, and waited, and thought, now what do I do? I may have to go call someone, this man has just dropped off and died while I'm sitting here. I wonder how they will write this one up?

But within a few minutes, he awoke and just kept on speaking right where he left off. Narcolepsy he said! We get the obituary finished and he said, oh because it's Lent, we are not able to put flowers in the church. Really? No Flowers! That was so unlike my mother, she always had fresh flowers in the house. I should have said, I think we will just do the service at the funeral home. But because we had never spoken about it, we just assumed that mom would want a church service, after all she was raised Catholic; she did go to church more than just at Easter and Christmas…so that is what we did.

The date was Tuesday, March 18th 1986. Mom was only just 62. Much too young. Just approaching Dad's retirement. They were going to travel. They loved going places.

Later that same afternoon their good friends, Joop and Ria Holst arrived from Hamilton. Joop had been friends with my Dad since they were young boys in the Netherlands. Joop and Dad had been next door neighbours since as long as they could remember. Mom and Ria had been girlfriends since Mom and Dad were married in 1946. We reminisced and talked and they promised to come back for Friday's service for Mom.

My Uncle Guus arrived from the Netherland on Thursday. It was good having him there. He was a sweet kind man, with a great sense of humour. He was grateful to be with us to share in the memories of his younger sister.

It was comforting to know he was there. We talked about family, and stories about when they were all younger. I was quite fond of this uncle, he had lots of stores and we enjoyed his presence. We had all been to the Netherlands and we did visit my aunt and uncle and we had a lovely time with them.

We received the autopsy report from Dr. H. Davidson on Thursday. It was determined that my mother had died at approximately 6 AM in the morning. She had died in her sleep of a massive heart attack. It was comforting to know that Mom had probably died instantly.

My room was across the hall, I had heard nothing.

The only Catholic funeral I had ever attended was for Bernadette Keuning. I had been asked to read the eulogy. The family had prepared a beautiful story, but no one was able to read it. They had called me and I said I would be honoured to do so.

Her funeral was held at St. Gregory's Catholic Church in Oshawa on the corner of Simcoe Street N and Adelaide. I did find it strange that her eulogy wasn't given in the church, but at the reception afterwards.

Another thing I had noticed was that often there were pregnant women at funerals.

So when someone is ready to leave their early home, we have another soul ready to be greeted by all who said goodbye to the original soul.

I must also say that my tante Ria and oom Joop have been sweet people to my brother and I when we were little. I always loved going with my parents to visit them when they lived in Stoney Creek. We would drive out to visit during peach season. We'd sit in the back yard, with a few baskets of peaches and enjoy the bounty of the fresh ripe fruit grown right in the Niagara area.

Chapter 5:

Mom's Funeral

Mom's Funeral. We wished we had done it differently, if only we had known what Mom's wishes were.

Father P. McCarrol arrived after 7PM on Thursday evening at the funeral home in Pickering Village; he was going to do prayers for Mom.

At that time I hadn't heard of Celebration of Life before. Had I known about it, things may have turned out differently?

Mom's funeral was going to be on Friday morning at 9AM since that was the time they did their regular service at St. Bernadette's Roman Catholic Church in Ajax.

The funeral coach picked us up early to take us to the church. I remember most details quite accurately; you see sad details of a cool but sunny Friday morning. I saw four of my co-workers arrive just before 9AM. It was as if I was watching a movie. Surreal!

Fr. McCarrol started his service; we were sitting right in front of him that morning. He mentioned that he was dedicating the service to my Mother, Laurentia Leone Maria Vroklage Spaans. And a few of her friends and our neighbours had bought Prayer Cards. (That was really the important part of his service.) We sat through a service that only mentioned her name a couple of times. There was nothing special mentioned about my mother, that she had a husband or 2 children or that she was a grandmother, a sister etc. It was the coldest unfeeling church service, which was supposed to celebrate Mom's life. There was nothing personal mentioned, no stories and to top it off, no flowers. I swore to myself, that if I ever did follow through and become a minister, I would never be so arrogant as to ignore the grieving family's wishes, of a person who had just died. It just wasn't right.

-0-0-0-

I blame the church for not acknowledging my Mom, and the funeral home for not telling me that the church wouldn't be doing a special service for my Mom. But what were we to think...we had no experience with funerals. And who would actually question a priest a man of spiritual and religious authority after all I was taught to respect them and not question them.

As a young girl, I would go to catechism classes in Whitby while I was living in Brooklin. The priest would pick us up at Mrs. Goodwin's house and drive down Hwy 12 to go to Whitby. I recall the drive to Whitby was a drive that I was used to. Father Leo Austin would pray in earnest to St. Christopher, all the way from Brooklin. And I would say to Fr. Austin, "You know Fr. Austin, you wouldn't have to pray so hard to St. Christopher if you didn't drive so fast." He would look at me, with a disgusting look, if eyes could kill. So my mother would receive another phone call to say, you tell your daughter to keep her opinions to herself.

So after being told often enough that you do not comment or ask questions of a priest, I guess I was finally stumped. I didn't know what to say or ask.

What a shame, that I didn't feel confident enough at that time to speak my mind. It was all about respect for the priest or my mother, the priest won.

There had been enough notes, letters and telephone calls to my mother for I had been quite the naughty student as far as Fr. Austin and catechism classes were concerned. Well I was grieving and I just hadn't been asking enough questions. After all it was Lent.

All I know is that it was a terrible ending for a beautiful mother, wife, sister and grandmother!

We had a reception at mom and dad's place on Billingsgate after the church service. We told stories, visited with each other and did our own celebration...***The moral of this story is, we are all going to die, one day. Talk to you loved ones and find out what you would like, otherwise you end up with what you get, and often it isn't what you want.***

If only I had been able to take time back to before Mom's passing. To be able to fix what I thought had not been right, and to show the proper respect for a mother who deserved better.

We first of all wouldn't have been so afraid to talk about death and dying. We would have known much better what Mom had wanted or what she would have liked. If she had known, she would have picked a time other than Lent to pass.

Chapter 6:

August 1995

When I was in grade 9, I was told I had Rheumatic Fever. I spend 2 weeks in the original old wooden hospital in Ajax. I had had sore joints, fever and a sore strep throat. After blood work had been done, my parents received a phone call from the family doctor to tell them the tests were back, I needed to go to the hospital for treatment of Rheumatic Fever.

 I was put to bed at the hospital in a cot similar to a camp cot. You see they had run out of beds and the only way I could be admitted was to sleep in a cot. So my parents said ok. I didn't care. I didn't really want to be there, so I thought of it as an adventure...camping inside. I spent most of the time sleeping and when I was awake, I could see young mothers walking by with big bellies...on one occasion I heard one say to the other, "My goodness, she is only 13." Every day penicillin shots were given to me in my cot. Well in my butt, while in my cot. lol

 I had no idea what they meant until I asked the nurse what they meant, and she told me that the only area where there had been room for a cot was in the maternity ward. So that was the story.

It was only 8 years earlier I had spent another week in the hospital in Bowmanville. Sore throat, high fever, this time it was Quinsy. Every day more penicillin shots!   And when the fever broke I could go home again, it was like déjà vu.

So let's forward to 1995, I am now 47 years old.

I've had pain in my body since at least 1986, but when I think about it, it has been even longer than that.

It wasn't until years later in March of 1995, that I was diagnosed with Fibromyalgia by Dr. Heather McDonald a Rheumatologist. I too had terrible pain everywhere. One only needs 11 of the 18 trigger points in diagnosing Fibro. I had 18 out of 18 active trigger points.

The exact cause of Fibromyalgia is not really known. It is suspected that it is due to infection, genetics and or trauma. The symptoms include widespread pain, fatigue, cognitive difficulties. Treatment includes medication and lifestyle changes. The early signs of Fibromyalgia are:

pain for 3 or more months, disturbed sleep, abdominal discomfort, profuse sweating, fibro fog, fatigue, insomnia, stiffness upon waking up, bloating, nausea and constipation, alternating with diarrhea IBS, tension headaches, jaw and facial tenderness, sensitivity to one or more of the following; odors, noise, bright lights, medications, certain foods, and cold. Feeling anxious or depressed, numbness or tingling in the face, arms hands, legs or feet. Increase in urinary urgency. Reduced tolerance for exercise, and muscle pain after exercise.

If fibromyalgia is a condition that affects the nervous system; as many doctors suggest it is, then it could be causing a breakdown between the nerves that control the esophagus and the brain. This would explain why people with fibromyalgia have a hard time swallowing. Their brain can't control the muscles in the esophagus as it normally would.

Some was from the surgery I had, a Bilateral Subcutaneous Mastectomy...and the reconstruction later contributed to the pain, the physical trauma to my body, and the brutal assault suffered in the beginning of March in 1986. Also the conditions at home in my case, living with a practicing alcoholic was difficult to deal with. He also had a hard time keeping his violent hands to himself.

I spoke to my doctor about the Fibromyalgia diagnosis, and asked him if my Mother could also have had Fibro as well. Considering that she had 3 years of intensive pain that never really left her body. It was possible.

At the same time, Bill Bowers who I had met in November had also received the diagnosis that he had diabetes. At the beginning of his diagnosis, he spent a week at Ruddy Hospital in Whitby, in a diabetic coma. Doctors had asked me to call his parents to have them come to the hospital to see their son. There was a chance he wasn't going to make it. But as luck would have it...he survived.

There was certain closeness because of these life altering situations with our health. Bill asked me to marry him Easter Sunday of 1995.

It was an unexpected question, I had only known him about 4 or 5 months, and I said I needed to think about it. After numerous discussions about marriage, I agreed. I truly believe it wasn't because of a love relationship for either one as I look back. It had more to do with a security of two people with health issues going forward together because it was thought to be easier and more supportive.

On August the 27th we married with about 100+ people present at the Treehouse in Ajax. We had a lovely ceremony officiated by Rev. Glen Jackson, it also included the healing circle women from my group. They drummed on native drums and sang. We had a program to tell who was who, and what the various aboriginal songs and poems meant. It was different! Rhoda Pickering and Alan Neilson stood up for us.

Dad and my aunt Nel, my cousin Paul Spaans came with his then girlfriend Lyda were there from the Netherlands, Bill's parents Sam and Vi Bowers my new in-laws all enjoyed the wedding. They had 5 daughters Sandra, Wanda, Brenda, Tammy and Tracey and a son Bill. My son Peter walked me down the aisle, my nieces, Sarah and Holly were bridesmaids and Bill's granddaughter Sarah was a flower girl. It was a perfect day. I loved them all. I now had a huge family.

Bill was a quiet, gentle guy. When I asked if he had a drinking problem, it was no. On our wedding night my girlfriend Trish

Clifford and my brother Pete, came back to the apartment to read cards, chat and have a nightcap. Although at the wedding he knocked back quite a few. He said it gave him courage to speak to people.

In hindsight which has 20/20 vision we should never have married. I think I had made a hasty decision. He had problems working as a mechanic. He would often get cellulites in his legs from bumping against the hoist.

I would always find out after the fact that he had bought something he wanted, not necessarily needed. He was careless with money, and I didn't realize I would be in for a hard ride as far as money was concerned.

During that first year Bill's Dad came down with Fibrosis of the Lungs, it was from particles that had been inhaled. Brake dust was probably the culprit from the time he ran a service station with his son and from the days of working at the Foundry in Bowmanville with malleable iron.

Bill bought a $10,000 tool chest at work and paid weekly for it. A nice set of golf clubs, with my credit card, motorcycles, and other toys. When I would say, hey it's rent day...he didn't hear me, so I would pay the rent. He had a white truck that he refinished, it looked awesome, but he would rather put the money into his truck that was called the 'white stallion' and ignore the rent it was at that time. The financial burden was laid at my feet. If we went out, he paid. It kept up appearances.

During this time I was also going to school, I spent 1999 at Scarborough Hospital, General Division doing a CAPPE Unit. We were renting a big house with a lady and her daughter during this time

I spent my own money, eventually I bought a nice house in 2001 with help from Vi and

Dad. Bill was going to be more involved in the running and paying of what needed to be paid. Things were going to be a little better and more stable I hoped.

Bill worked as a mechanic during the day and since he had invested money into bar in Ajax, he was the man about town. He'd come home and clean up and head to the bar. Well having a bar is all good and well, if you don't have another job to do, and you have a partner who is honest in his dealings. Before we knew it there were difficulties getting statements from the partner. The office was such a mess, you couldn't find anything. So if I had asked Bill if he had his shit together, he honestly would have said NO!

So the moral of this story is, if you have a business, you need a Will for sure as well as Power of Attorneys. Especially if you have diabetes, on 4 needles a day.

We never should have owned a bar, it was too much work for someone who was working already and I was a student…so the timing and the responsibility was too much.

By the time 2000 rolled around, I was laid up with terrible pain in my arms. There was also tingling, and numbness in my upper arm and the symptoms were annoying. An appointment was made for me at St Mikes in their neurology department and it was determined it was the start of Spinal Stenosis. Stenosis means narrowing, so this meant that there was a narrowing of the inside of the vertebrae, and it is through this cannel that the spinal cord runs. As it narrows, it starts to touch the spinal cord and it starts to damage it. The tingling and numbness is the damage that you're feeling or not feeling. It would need to be addressed sometime in the future.

Chapter 7:

9/11 2001

It was my birthday as it was every September 11th. Just like any other birthday until September 11th 2001! The world would never be the same again. We all remember what we were doing and where we were.

We were experiencing a day like any other. I was having a cup of coffee on the deck. It was bright and sunny. Bill was at work. My mother in law Viola Bowers, who now lived with us, was up early too because of therapy. She was living with us after her husband Sam had died and she had suffered a stroke in the spring of 2001.

As an aside going back to what had happened to Vi; she had laid on the bathroom floor for quite a few hours. It wasn't until her daughter Tammy had found her and called an ambulance. She was taken to Ajax Pickering General Hospital and then transferred to St. Michael's Hospital in Toronto. After numerous days there she had pressure on her brain that needed to be relieved.

Vi did have surgery to relieve the pressure in her brain, and fortunately she was able to survive. Although she had a number of issues afterwards, which made it impossible for her to look after herself and live alone.

 We invited Mom to live with us since we did have room. She arrived at our house around the middle of August, and we were working out the various aspects of her care when that terrible day arrived, 9/11!

Mom had been picked up at 8:30 AM by her daughter Wanda, who had taken her to physiotherapy that morning. And I had a 9AM appointment with a rep from one of the agencies which helped look after people with impairments from stroke. We needed to get some help in to look after Mom.

At 9AM the doorbell rang, and a very shocked young woman stood there and said, "Do you have your TV on?" And I said no. Come in.

I then found out the something terrible had happened in New York City at the World Trade Centre. I turned on CNN in time to see something terrible was about to happen again when the second airplane flew into the Towers. It was incredulous.

We sat and watched and never really did have that meeting we were supposed to have.

Since the turn of the millennium *2000, we have had a number of frightening events; that we had to sit up and take notice. George Bush was President* of the United States of America, and it wasn't likely that they would let it go. Many people died a terrible horrific event that affected the whole world. But what happened in 2001 on 9/11 was something the world had never witnessed before. The over 3000 office workers in the Trade Centre and the front line workers, who saved many from the towers, ended up dying that day! I wonder how many were prepared and had their Power of Attorneys and their Wills prepared?

I know that it seems like a callous question, but it shows how quickly something can happen out of the blue to take your life away and change the lives of your family! Instantaneously! No negotiating or opportunity to make it better or to write that will or power of attorney.

I would think that not even half would have been prepared. According to the statistics; and the thing are we never know when the need for these documents comes into play. You could live to be 105, 75, or become ill at a young age and need specialized care. In the event of the latter, you need to have the Power of Attorney for Health Care.

The other thing is you really can't wait; these documents need to be prepared while you are of sound mind.

Chapter 8:

Piet – October 2002

Doctors had said that Dad could expect 6 months. He never complained. He was uncomfortable from time to time; we reminded him that he could ask for something to ease pain. And then he would ask. I reminded him, that if he was in pain at night and he couldn't sleep, to ask for a pain killer, he certainly didn't over do it. He wanted to stay as alert as possible and not miss anything.

In September he still went apple picking at Windemere Farms with a group from the palliative care unit. That had been a wonderful experience for him. He had said he wanted to use these apples for apple crisp for his grandson Peter and his wife Tammy when the new baby came. This was now the second time in our family that we were losing a parent and grandparent and we had a pregnant momma in the family.

The first time, it was Jackie my brother's wife who was expecting their second child; and this time it was Tammy, my youngest son's wife, also with their second child.

In October he was still enjoying visitors. I usually came for a visit in the afternoon. We had many long talks. He was happy that he was here as his life was drawing to a close.

Thanksgiving was also in October, and that day, Ann Hooper came for a visit to the hospital. We had made arrangements for Bill and I to have Thanksgiving dinner with Dad. The dinner was a traditional Turkey Dinner with all the trimmings. He enjoyed it very much and so did we. We were grateful to be able to spend some enjoyable hours with him. Dad could be quite humorous, and he didn't mind a joke or a good story. Thanksgiving had been better than we ever could have hoped for.

We were grateful that Dad had come back to Canada when he wasn't feeling well. I felt so blessed that was here with us. It would have been such a sad situation had he not been able to fly back in February. But God had heard my prayers and made it possible for Dad to still make it back to us.

Quite often on Friday afternoons I would attend the Chapel service with Dad, it was 18 years ago, I can still picture the chaplain's face, but for the life of me, I can't remember his name. He was also a very nice man, and he had introduced dad to angels. He always took the time to speak.

Knowing what we went through with my Mother unexpected passing, I knew we wouldn't have to experience such emotional pain by having to do it while you were suffering the shock of losing a loved one. So one day while I was visiting Dad, he said, 'Go to that funeral home near where you live and plan and pay for the funeral out of my account."

If you are able to plan and prepay the funeral service, that is wonderful. Funeral homes don't mind at all if you pay in advance. Your money is put in trust. It is said that if you prepay, all your worries about a funeral will be done and over with. You have made all the decisions, Bravo for doing this.

Dad said that it would be less painful to do it before he died. The emotions won't be as high as it will be on the day that your loved one dies. So the next time I was out, I made a trip over to the funeral home and made the arrangements.

Michael Bishop and I have discussed death hundreds of times over a coffee in the cafeteria at Lakeridge Health. We have spoken about preparing for a funeral, but this time it was for Dad's and I realized what he had really wanted was a Celebration of Life. So that is what we planned.

I remember Dad saying to me, I've got to meet and talk to Michael, the chaplain here at the hospital, and I really like him, and he understands me. Michael knows what I mean when I speak to him. So it was a good fit.

"See if Michael will do my funeral for me." Dad asked ok Cath? And of course Michael agreed.

Michael understood people, and could relate to them so well. Over the years Michael had said he liked my Dad. Maybe he saw something in Dad that made him comfortable, as if he was talking to his own father.

When the day came that Dad had passed away, Michael was there for me. I didn't have to go look for someone besides myself to do his funeral. I knew that Michael would do a good job and it would be personal, and I didn't worry about it because I knew we were in good hands. Michael and I spoke a few days before the funeral and we planned out how it would go, my cousin Mia went with me to talk to Michael.

You want to have pallbearers...you pick out 6 and 2 spares...

Dad had made some suggestions as to who would be the pall-bearers, and we asked 2 honourary pallbearers. They were 2 delightful friends one of which was Joop Holst, a friend and neighbour of Dad since they were young boys, and the other Luke Segers, who had been a family friend for about 50 years. They were about the same age as Dad, they didn't have to lift or carry the casket. They led the other pall bearers. I was reminded that I would most likely have to bring some clothes to the funeral home, since you only have PJ's with you in the hospital. Everything was organized and paid for ahead of time. I ordered the flowers, on Monday afternoon from Albert Segers in Pickering who Dad had known for years, he was Luke's older brother.

 My cousin Mia Spaans arrived from the Netherlands to be here for her Uncles Piet's funeral. Mia was a wonderful support for me. She had been here a few months earlier with her husband Bob to visit us and to spend time with her uncle. Mia also brought the music that Dad had requested to be played at his funeral the elusive tango.

For ministers, clergy, or funeral directors to organize a funeral it is a lot like preparing any other production…I'm always drawn back to my TV days, preparing a show or a program. What do you want to tell? So you have the introduction, the middle with a bridge to the end of the story or the Committal of a funeral service.   It is not so much different than preparing a wedding, a party…it has a beginning, middle and an end. So it's a matter of getting the material out there. Hold your composure, and don't let your emotions get tangled into the content.

As the celebrant, you will often see a member of the immediate family weep. It is a heart breaker for us too. Because we know that you are hurting. Your dear one is not ever coming back...and if we let that thought get to us, we are a goner too...

That is why it is not (I believe) healthy for a minister to do the funeral of a very close relative. The thing is the funeral is done for the living. And as I am part of the living and in the case of my father, I too needed that funeral to be able to go on.

So when my father died, I decided not to *do* his funeral. As a matter of fact, I didn't even speak at his funeral. There were a number of reasons that I couldn't do it as well. All I remember now is that, I was feeling such pain from the loss but also body pain from Fibromyalgia. And the other thing was, my hands and feet were tingling and I had no idea what that was about, and I didn't want to take the chance that I would pass out or keel over while speaking.

I had selected 6 Pallbearers and 2 Honorary Pallbearers. I needed to ask them if they would do this for my Dad. They all said yes.

The flowers that had been ordered had arrived in time for the visitation. A beautiful blanket of salmon and orange flowers, roses and cream coloured carnations as well as greenery, it was spectacular. I perhaps did go a little overboard, but for me it was meant for Mom and Dad's reunion in Heaven...remember her funeral was in Lent. No Flowers. It still annoys me today about the no flowers, why it would have been much easier if they had said, no chocolate at the reception that, I could have lived with that.

Michael did a wonderful job, and I was never questioned by anyone as to why I didn't do Dads funeral. He was happy to do it for me, he had gotten to know Dad, and he could relate well to him and tell his own stories from when he and Dad had spoken in the hospital. He could also relate to what Mia had shared with him while Dad had lived in the Netherlands.

Another reason Dad's funeral was nice for us, was because we had planned it that way. Because some of the worry of organizing it had already been done, and we knew exactly what we wanted. That ended up saving us time and a lot of extra grief. We knew since the day that we had my Mother's funeral, that Dad's would be organized more carefully by us instead of leaving it up to a total stranger. Piet himself had been involved in the planning. It was personal, a bit of humour thrown in, and the music...you couldn't help but smile.

We of course had a very good respect for the permanence of death, Michael and I, as celebrants still mourn like others, and we continue to deal and counsel others who are grieving.

-o-o-o-

If you are stuck with your grief, and it is lasting longer than what you think is normal. Speak to someone who is able to help you navigate through it. Sometimes we end up in a rut, and we just can't figure our way through.

I have included some reference material at the back of the book. There is also a questionnaire to help your family decide your final moments on the earth, should you be hospitalized and need palliative care. It is always recommended that you have a Power of Attorney for Health Care and another POA for property.

It is much easier for someone to actually go to the funeral home prior to the death of a loved one, make the arrangements that he or she would like to see happen for his/her funeral service. Pay for the service and forget about it. It is done, it is planned.

I spoke with the funeral director about my Dad. I told him, as of recently he has become quite intrigued by angels, and the funeral director brought out a condolence book with angels on the cover. We wrote the obituary but left out the date. All the travel logistics were arranged, Dad would be picked up from Lakeridge Whitby Ruddy Hospital, a long-term care/and palliative care hospital. I talked to the funeral director about the service, and we wrote down that Rev. Michael Bishop was going to be doing Dad's service. I just needed to confirm that.

Dad had told me the music he wanted played; I would make sure that I brought the CD's to the funeral home. So the first piece was Josh Groban's 'To Where You Are', a beautiful song about someone who has passed and the singer wants to know where they are, because he still feels her around. 'Fly me up to where you are...you are watching me from up above?'

Then also the hymn, In the Garden was chosen by Jackie Dad's daughter in law. The next song was, 'Adios Nonino', a beautiful piece of music from an Argentinean composer. It was actually a story about the Argentinean song, Adios Nonino. The original story was about a man saying goodbye to his grandson. But this time it was for a daughter saying goodbye to her father.

It was played at the wedding of the Dutch Crown Prince Willem-*Alex*ander married Maxima, on the 2nd of February 2002 in Amsterdam in a Civil Ceremony.

Last but not least ending with the Celine Deon song composed and written by David Foster, 'The Prayer...I pray you'll be our eyes, and watch us where we go.' A beautiful song! It was played as the guests were leaving the chapel out to the reception hall, where we waited for the casket to be loaded into the hearse. The hearse made a short trip to Thornton Cemetery where Dad was cremated.

My father was an auto mechanic but he was also quite a good musician and accordion player, and as you may know, the accordion lends itself nicely to tango music. Adios Nonino was a beautiful tango. It had been composed by an Argentinean musician Astor Piazzolla for the passing of his father, and played for the wedding of The Dutch crown prince and his fiancé a banker Maxima Zorreguieta ... Maxima was saying good bye to her dad. You see during the Dirty War her father was found to have been a war criminal and the Dutch Government and Royal family didn't want him attending the wedding. So neither Maxima's father nor mother would be attending the wedding. With her mother not wishing to attend without her husband; there was apparently a special gathering for her parents afterwards in the Netherlands.

My father had said to me one day when I had asked him if he was satisfied with his life. And part of his answer was he had wished that he lived long enough to see the Crown Prince marry Maxima. He had watched it on Television in the Netherlands a week before coming to Canada.

Chapter 9:

SARS

This viral respiratory disease was caused by a SARS-associated coronavirus. It was first identified at the end of February 2003 during an outbreak that emerged in China and spread to 4 other countries. The World Health Organization (WHO) coordinated the international investigation with the assistance of the Global Outbreak Alert and Response Network (GOARN) and worked closely with health authorities in affected countries to provide epidemiological, clinical and logistical support and to bring the outbreak under control.

SARS was certainly explained as a serious virus. People around the world died. People with SARS suffered, tremendously and many health care workers and a number of SARS Specialists were claimed by this virus as well.

Severe Acute Respiratory Syndrome (SARS)

By having a minister officiate or celebrate, you know and can have the confidence that they have been trained to perform the duties that are needed for a funeral or celebration of life service.

They also have the training to be empathetic and sensitive to the needs of their client. In most cases they have had a death in their own family so they have a good idea how hurt and upset that their clients are.

When they have the complete story and all the information they can put together a plan without a lot of waiting, wondering and more phone calls. They are professionals who in most cases know what they are doing.

When Dad was in the hospital in palliative care, a month before he passed away he went on a little bus trip to Windermere Orchard and farm to pick a bag of apples. He was so happy to have picked the apples. He said to me the following day, do you think you can keep these apples until the baby comes. I'd like you to make an apple crisp for them to celebrate.

Well I wasn't sure if the apples would last that long. I put the apples loosely in the crisper in the bottom of the refrigerator and honest to God; the apples were great and still ready to be made into an apple crisp. So on the appointed day, I made the apple crisp, and brought it to Pete and Tammy's house on the day we met Kelsi.

Severe acute respiratory syndrome (SARS) came to unburden it's self in February of 2003. I remember it well since I had a pregnant daughter in law that was due to give birth to her second baby early April. It was a scary time for them for sure, as it was for many.

At that particular time I was an On Call Chaplain at Lakeridge Health in Oshawa Hospital. When it was announced that this new virus caused many heavy duty breathing issues for patients,

We were sent an email by Michael Bishop who was the lead Chaplain for Lakeridge Health at that time, that we were to remain at home and not come in for any reason, No visiting patients, no to everything. As a matter of fact, he was the only one of the spiritual care team who were allowed to go in to visit with patients, as was a Catholic priest who attended to patients of the Catholic denomination.

April 2nd Tammy and Peter Hansen gave birth to their second daughter our beautiful Kelsi. I would have loved to see her, but that was impossible. We had to wait to visit until she was sent home and out of quarantine. I think we went to visit 10 or 14 days later. That gorgeous little one winked at me the first time I looked at her.

I arrived with a fresh baked apple crisp, made from the apples picked by Kelsi's great Opa Piet Spaans.

-0-0-0-

After Dad died, I really wasn't feeling very good. I was feeling like I had no energy, my hands and feet were tingling and prickly, I had no energy to even walk around. I spent most of my days in bed, sleeping. Everyone was sure that I was just depressed, but this was going on for a bit too long. I had been to the doctor, had blood work done, but I never heard back from it. So I assumed that everything was ok.

In the mean time my boys were calling and saying don't you think it's about time we bury Opa? I said, I really feel terrible I just can't do it now. We did have a plot for burying Dad with Mom, but I kept postponing it.

My girlfriend Lynda Liscio called one day and we talked and she said she would go with me to my doctor. She drove out from Brampton and took me to see my doctor in Ajax. Because I had not had blood results I went for blood work again, and we decided that maybe a mild antidepressant would help. So off I went to do blood work. Well when the blood work came back it came back that my B-12 was so low, it was nearly off the chart. They called me and had me come back. It turned out the blood work had been filed before the doctor saw it, and it was incorrectly filed. The pain in my hands and feet were explained by the low levels of B-12. Within a couple of weeks the energy improved but the pain in my hands and feet stayed.

We made plans to bury Dad's ashes with Mom's at Groveside Cemetery in Brooklin, on Hwy 12. The day arrived and our family had a private internment for Dad and the boys Opa. It was a sunny June afternoon; I celebrated Dad's internment and reunited my parents. I was happy to get it done. The ceremony was good for all of us. Mom and Dad were now together again, the way it should have been.

By 2004 I had reached my goal, my courses all finished. I was doing On Call at Lakeridge Health since the end of 2002. I was doing pulpit supply at Scugog Island; I was also licensed by the Province of Ontario to officiate weddings. Because of Fibromyalgia

I was not able to work full time. And I never knew from day to day how I would be feeling.

Chapter 10:

Viola –September 2007
Lively Events at a Funeral

When the date and time had come for the funeral, we were prepared for amazing things to happen. My mother in law Viola Bowers had passed away from a stroke and the funeral was being planned at Oshawa Funeral Services on King Street East in Oshawa. The family had worked hard pulling pictures together of Viola with her children and husband Sam. The visitation was awesome; so many people came to express their condolences at the funeral home. Viola being the one who loved parties, gatherings, and I think she even enjoyed a nice funeral she would have been happy with the turn out.

On the day of the funeral I had made sure I was at the funeral home early enough. I met my sister in laws outside. We chatted briefly and suddenly my two arm canes were swept away...and we laughed and someone said, that's mom...she's here.

Bill and I had arrived early to meet my sister in laws. Sandra Lamb, Wanda Bowers, Brenda Scheepers, Tammy Bowers and Tracey Bryant Bowers.

The funeral guests came into the chapel and sat down, Vi's grandson Tyler (Tracey's son) was able to attend from his group home with his 2 staff members. He had been very close to his Grandma and Grandpa.

At the appointed time, I started the service, 'We have come together to celebrate the life of Viola Bessie Johnston Bowers"....and as I was into the opening paragraph of what I was about to say, a picture that was hanging on the wall behind me, fell to the floor.

There were awes, and gasps, snickers and within a few seconds I said "I do believe that Vi is here for her farewell party. And the chapel broke into wonderful laughter and a few clapped. And when they settled down I continued…It was a lovely funeral! We did indeed celebrate Vi that day. We had asked Dale Gray to sing and he did a beautiful job singing You Raise Me Up. Sandra's and Rod Lamb's son Stephen and daughter Samantha came forward and read the eulogy…Grandma Vi would have been proud of you.

It went the way it was supposed to. Vi wouldn't miss a good party for all the tea in China.

They had a lovely reception for Vi downstairs in the lounge, and there were all kinds of finger foods, and sandwiches, pastries and cookies. When I finally got to sit down with a cup of coffee, it was nice for me to reminisce with the family and friends. I was nearly finished my coffee, when I saw something really bazaar happen. I had just put the cup on the saucer, and it was about 10 inches away from the edge of the table. When suddenly, without anyone touching or hitting the cup, it flew across the table and landed on the floor. When I witnessed this, I thought, Vi has certainly made an appearance today. She did after all like a good funeral. In that respect she was a lot like me.

A couple of years later, I celebrated the service for Viola's mother Vera Johnston was nearly 102nd years young.

Chapter 11:

Time for a new hip or two

I was lucky that my friend and roommate Trish Clifford brought me to the hospital in Oshawa for surgery early in the morning. I was living in Lindsay and it was quite a drive to get there, early in the morning. I had moved to Trish's because I couldn't walk stairs anymore, and since she lived in a bungalow, for me it was the perfect solution, I was so happy when she asked if I wanted to move to Lindsay. Now a couple of times I have been in the hospital, and I have been feeling pretty punky.

The first few days after getting my hips replaced, I spent most of the time sleeping. The first hip I felt pretty weak and tired. When the nurse went to get me out of bed to go to the washroom I nearly fainted. I said to the nurse, I think I am going to pass out. Oh dear, don't worry, everyone says that. But the thing was, I really did feel like I was passing out, and as I started to step forward, I started to go down. I said sorry, but I am going to pass out. I couldn't hear anything, my hearing had that 'Wah Wah, Wah" sound with the vibration that goes with it and the nausea...down I went!

Well they tested my blood, and although I hadn't lost a lot of blood during the surgery, my hemoglobin numbers were very low as was my blood pressure, and a blood transfusion was ordered.

And I thought, I'm happy I have a PoA and my Will done.

The thing is, you don't plan to have something go wrong, but from time to time, things do go wrong. We think we are in control, but are we really? I had asked my girlfriend Lynda Liscio and her husband to help me put a POA together and a Will, just in case. It made me feel prepared for the surgery, and I didn't have to worry in case something did go wrong.

So you do what needs to be done. You prepare a Power of Attorney for your Health Care ahead of time, so that when it is needed you will have it. As in my case, it wasn't needed, but in the event that I had my heart stop, or I developed a blood clot...they would be aware of what they needed to do for me.

Each time I had surgery for my hips, I took my Power of Attorney with me, and I said, please put it in my file, and they did. It was signed and properly witnessed and legal.

o-o-o-o

You see, I will not be spending weeks on a ventilator or other piece of equipment that is going to keep me alive and have me hooked up to something for the rest of my life. Eventually my family would be asked to turn the machine off, and I didn't want to have that happen. I wanted no feelings of guilt afterwards for my sons.

I like to get out, do things, visit, and shop. Write, play piano, make jewelry, and write a blog and a book, so machines would be in the way. So I need, and I do have a Power of Attorney that states that fact, I have a DNR which means, **do not resuscitate** in the case of a horrific life altering problem.

You are usually heavily sedated when you are put on a ventilator. I believe you can hear who is speaking to you, but you can't answer. It would have been good to live to be 84, but if I'm not that old yet, they can make me comfortable and let me slip away.

I had spent another 2 weeks after the first 4 or 5 days in rehab exercising my new hip. I was lucky to have Michael Bishop come to visit me during that time...I witnessed for myself the caliber of chaplain that he was. A man of Christ and compassion! He was such a good listener, because there were a few times, I felt so terrible that he was able to talk me down, and made me feel that all would be alright. All in all it was a good experience all around. That grinding pain in my hip was gone. I just had to get the power back in my leg, once I was able to put weight on it again. The next few months went fairly well enough that when it was time to get the second hip done, I went without worry.

I was given a second surgery date for November and I went back for my second hip. I knew what to expect and at that time. My roommate and friend Trish Clifford had brought me to the hospital and got me settled first thing on that Friday morning.

I was blessed to have my friends and colleagues visit and bring me spiritual care especially on days that the pain was too much.

And after the hospital stay was over I had no sooner been home, when I had to go to Peterborough for my disability hearing for my CPPD. The drive to the hotel with Trish was exhausting, I was still in so much pain, I was breaking out in a cold sweat and I could hardly talk from the pain. The committee took a good look at me and granted me the disability.

I was very lucky to have so much help from my friends.

I was so fortunate that I was able to get my hips done within a fairly short period of time. We are lucky in Canada to have a health care system that looks after its residents. Not all provinces have that luxury.

My Friend Michael, My Brother!

Through-out my book I have mentioned Michael Bishop, my friend and adopted brother. Everyone should have a caring soul such as Michael for a brother.

Here is a glimpse into Michael in his own words. He has been such a blessing to me. When my father was in hospital, Michael was his chaplain at Lakeridge Oshawa. They got to know each other and finally Michael did his Celebration of Life. And in all honesty it was a lovely sendoff for a special man. He is so much more than a funeral celebrant. You can talk to this man!

In Michael's Own Words

In my working career I have been involved in many areas. As a minister and Chaplain I have found one area to be especially close to my heart. Caring for those who have lost a loved one or are in the process of grieving has become very dear to me. In reflection, it's because it is a time in life where feelings are real and there is little time for trivial things that can consume life.

My personality is such that I find it an honour to be included in a time where memories and capturing a person's life is so important. A funeral is a sad occasion but a special time to reflect and celebrate a person's life. Tears, yes but also a time of joy in recalling moments shared by a family. My advice to anyone facing such a special time is to find someone who truly cares and is gifted in celebrating a life. It is one of those unique moments that cannot be treated lightly. When a family is in a time of loss, a skilled officiant is invaluable to ensure your loved one's memory is honoured and accurately reflected.

Nothing is more frustrating to me than to be at a memorial time and have it be a very "religious" event and to find out that the person being remembered had little or no faith. Words and readings shared need to reflect and capture the essence of who your loved was and still is to you. Most families have someone they know who can share a memory packed eulogy but my opinion is that someone is still needed to graciously conduct the ceremony from the beginning to the end. Family members need to grieve and an officiant is important.

Most funeral homes are quite skilled in managing the logistics of a service and will ensure a smooth transition from the initial visitation time and the actual memorial time. It is hard when you have lost a loved one to think of all the details that are important. If there will be a casket, will it be open or closed?

Will there be a burial and if so who will be pallbearers. Some want to see the casket lowered into the grave while others do not. Some want special music played during the visitation as well as during the memorial and some choose at the cemetery as well.

(Photo: Michael Bishop with his mother when she was visiting from out west.)

I focus in caring for others - have focused on the palliative person and his or her family. We know that personal experience is an important factor in being able to have a compassionate heart. My own life has been one of deep valleys and mountain top moments. I have walked through the valley of death many times and am still here. I cannot explain why one passes through near death and another does not. I began a BLOG awhile back with the hope that it can inspire and encourage others. All are welcome to come and read and interact through comments. It can be found at www.bishopsthoughts.com I also am beginning an online grief support network. For further information you can connect to me through email at bishopsthoughts@mail.com

Chapter 12:

Mitral Valve

I had met Lorne on line on E-Vow a subsidiary of Plenty of Fish. We were both more or less on the last attempt to find the perfect partner, and I happened to see Lorne's profile picture. I thought, hmm, handsome, nice colour shirt on him, and his face drew me in, and I sent him a message. "Old and crusty looking for same" was the profile line Lorne used, and I thought, he doesn't look too old, I'll send him a message. He answered, and that was it. I never had another date with anyone.

(photo: Lorne King)

Dating as an adult has its advantages; but the head games that some people played, was too much, and when you break up with them some become stalkers. It was enough to make me nearly give up all together.

On March 8th Lorne and I met in person, after I attended a funeral in Ajax. We met in Port Perry at the Halibut House. We had fish and chips for dinner that night. He had a previous engagement, and he left early to do that. We had decided that we did like each other, and we would see each other again.

Lorne reminded me of my Dad a little bit, he was soft spoken, a gentleman, the way he says 'hello' to me when he comes in the door. By the following weekend we had made a date to meet in Lindsay. He got a hotel room he wanted to take his time, and not pressure either one of us. Just talk. We spend time together that evening, talking and drinking coffee, finding out about each other. I went home, and he stayed.

Over the next few months, we enjoyed motorcycle rides on his Suzuki Belvedere C90 1500 cc a very comfortable bike, our first ride was from Lindsay where I was living to Bobcaygeon to the Kawartha Dairy for ice cream, and we brought a container of Death by Chocolate home…decadent, rich and totally delicious.

We celebrated our birthdays, and I was spoiled with a Mandarin dinner, roses and a nice card that reflected a lovely sentiment and I had a feeling that this was a keeper. We had enjoyed going to the cottage up north in Dunchurch and all was good.

There was an addition being built onto the cottage and it was going to be comfortable now that it was going to be twice as big. By the time Christmas rolled around, I was excited to have Lorne over and I had invited Cynthia a friend from Toronto. I had made a nice Turkey dinner for Christmas and I got it all prepared and on the table when suddenly I said to Lorne and Cynthia, I don't know what is wrong, but I feel horrible. I was exhausted, I coughed for quite some time, and I said, I feel sick. I went to bed without dinner. I felt terrible for bailing on them, but I couldn't hold my head up, and I was out like a light once I got into bed.

I slept for 3 days, and this lovely man, stayed with me to make sure I was ok. He was off on Christmas holidays, so fortunately he was able to stay and not miss work. After the 3rd day I was feeling better. New Years Eve we went out with Trish and her friend to a dinner dance in Peterborough. I was feeling better, but had no energy.

Happy New Year! 2015 had got nicely started when one morning around the 24th I woke up and I could not breathe. It was a regular singing lesson that day, and I thought, instead of going singing I better call and cancel and make a doctor's appointment instead.

This I did and I was shocked to find out what was going on with my heart. Here I had found the love of my life, and now my heart was giving up. How fair was that?

When I got out of bed that morning, I realized I was quite sick. I had a hard time breathing and I was so pooped out, I tried walking upstairs, and when I realized I couldn't walk the stairs, I decided to call my doctor's office instead. To make a long story short, Rosemary the secretary said to me why I can give you an appointment for February 8th, and I said to her, no, I will be dead by then. Oh it's that bad? Yes I said, I can barely breathe, she said come right down!

My doctor's office was in Brooklin, and I lived in Lindsay. I hadn't been able to find a doctor in Lindsay after being there nearly 5 years. Dr. P. Laroche was a good hour's drive from my home but, I was determined to make it. My gut told me to get there as soon as possible.

When I arrived at the Medical Centre, Rosemary took me right in.

Within a few minutes Dr. Laroche came in. I said to him I felt terrible, I thought I had the flu, but I could hardly breathe...He said let's take a listen. He took his stethoscope and listened to my chest. He stood back and said, "There is a problem."

He was quite sure that I had a prolapsed mitral valve with regurgitation. I asked him to write it down. I was shocked. He said I needed a cardiologist and he was going to put the referral out to 3 cardiologists in the area. Whoever contacts you first, that is where you go, he said. I went home and that afternoon Dr.Kumar's office called.

I called Lorne and told him what had happened. The following day Lorne drove me to Dr Kumar's office in Whitby for an echocardiogram and stress test. And indeed my sharp family physician had called it right. I was indeed in trouble with my heart and with fluid in my lungs. Before we left Dr. Kumar's office, he spoke with us and had already made arrangements for me at St. Michael's Hospital in Toronto, and had lined me up with a fabulous young cardiologist.

St. Michael's is a state of the art hospital right downtown. I was blessed to be sent there!

The following week I was in to see Dr. Akshay Bagai, an interventional cardiologist at St. Michael's Hospital. He repeated of the same tests I had done at the cardiologist in Whitby …and back again 2 days later on Friday for and an transesophageal ultrasound of the heart in the morning and in the afternoon an angiogram. At the end of the day I was admitted and scheduled for surgery as soon as the fluid was cleared out of my lungs.

I had packed a bag in case I was going to be admitted, some personal stuff, toiletries and my Power of Attorney for Health Care.

After Lorne had left to go back home to his place, I was in my room and a nurse stopped in and she said, I will leave this with you and when you get a moment, please read it.

It was an 8 ½ x 11 inch booklet entitled Congestive Heart Failure. Up until that moment, I had been ok with what was going on, but when I read the title, I realized how much trouble I was really in. It scared me, and I burst into tears.

As a hospital chaplain I had prayed and talked to patients with the same diagnosis, not all of them made it. I remembered my first funeral, while I was a student. He didn't make it. And for a moment I was very afraid. And I thought what would I tell a patient?

Don't put the cart before the horse. Ask God to help heal you, and ask your friends and colleagues to pray for you.

This took a bit of doing but after ten or so days I was schedule for the 24th of February. I met Dr. David Latter who was a Mitral Valve surgeon and he came in a few days before surgery to explain what he was going to do.

My boyfriend Lorne King was there. We had found that we cared a lot for each other, and he wasn't running for the hills. I suppose we had a good idea who we were, and by the time this happened to me, his participation in my care, his concern certainly showed his good character. We had only known each other less than a year but we had talked about retirement together.

The day of surgery came. I was excited to get it done. What I had experienced at that hospital was phenomenal caring for patients, and I felt that I was in good hands and that I would be ok.

My friends Erik and Lynda Liscio were with me as well as Lorne. We waited together in the cardiac waiting area to be taken in for surgery. I was allowed to take my phone with me. While waiting for my surgery time my son called and my friend Michael Bishop called, he prayed for me. It was quite a send off...at the appointed time I was wheeled into the operating room. I said something like, yes let's do this.

It was a huge operating room. It held so much equipment, and so many doctors and nurses and technicians. They were all there for me. A doctor with a Greek sounding name held a huge book, my chart. He asked each individual technician and team leader if they were ready to go. He then asked me if it was ok if they could pray for me. I said yes please. And they did. I was so at ease. I felt ok...I wasn't scared, I knew the Almighty Physician was also present guiding each person's hand as well as Dr.

David Latter's hands. I totally trusted him. He knew what he was doing.

I had to choose between a mechanical valve and a porcine valve. There were advantages and disadvantages with both, but the decision I had made didn't need to be considered because when they open my chest for the open heart surgery he chose to repair my heart, which in hindsight was the correct and brilliant decision!!!

Dr. Latter and his team did good work that day. I survived.

The recovery was a piece of cake compared to how I had felt before. I was grateful for another chance at life. I had many people involved in my recovery. My eternal gratitude goes to Cynthia. She had offered her place for me to stay. I stayed with her after my release from the hospital. I was there for about a month. Her little dog Benji was my constant companion...he would lay on my bed, all day long, watching me, as if he knew what I needed. He was so gentle, never jumped on me, and by the end of the day, he was exhausted from watching, and he would stay with Cynthia. It was special, yes it was.

On my drive home from Toronto to Lindsay with Lorne, I saw the green coming out on the tree's the clouds and the sky was more beautiful than I had ever seen. The fields and meadows were so amazingly perfect I had never seen that before. Everything was more beautiful than I had ever remembered it. The music was brighter, the birds sang so sweetly and life was perfect.

It was the Rheumatic Fever that caused all of this.

My first doctor's appointment after the surgery was with Dr. Laroche when I was back in my own apartment. It was a week after my return home.

He said, "How are you?" I said, "I am so happy!" He stood back and looked and said, you know, every time I ask that question of an open heart patient, the answer is always 'happy' they don't say I'm fine, or I feel good, they say happy.

I truly believe that God has something to do with that. A person like me a minister, who has faith in God, believes in God, and believes that there is a divine happening that is mixed into the healing process. It is of God and of the doctors, the whole team that started with my family doctor.

He started the ball rolling. He did a good job in identifying the problem, and each individual who was involved in my care was so smart, brilliant, it all came together for me as it was ordained.

My Power of Attorney was not needed! But I had it; I was prepared, just in case.

I also believe that my personal relationship with God is of comfort to me, and that as well as my own personality gives me a responsibility to do something with it.

I tell my story. I implore people to do what they need to do so that they can live a good life.

I have been told, God isn't finished with me yet. Lorne says to me, 'I think you are connected to the man upstairs.' And I say, yes I am! He has kept me alive through a number of trials and tribulations, and I am here to play witness that God performs miracles every day.

Chapter 13:

Decompression Surgery

It was June I believe of 2017 when I started having very annoying symptoms from what I thought was Spinal Stenosis, I was falling, my feet were partly numb and I was very much off balance. I walked as if I was drunk, and there were a few other symptoms associated with my bowels, I won't go into detail. I spoke to Dr. Laroche about it and he wrote a note.

He said to me, if you were my family, I would be taking you to the ER and have you checked out. So I thanked him, took my note and went home. At this point Lorne and I were living in Markham. On weekends we were getting the cottage ready to move into at the end of September.

When I got home I called Lorne, and told him about my doctor's appointment. He came home around 5, and we headed to Markham Stouffville Hospital's ER.

We saw a doctor who checked me out, I gave her the note from my family doctor, and she ordered a Cat Scan for my spine.

In an hour we had an idea that there was a problem, she didn't elaborate, she said she wanted me to see an orthopedic spine surgeon, she said he was very good. The following week I saw Dr. Kevin Koo, and he looked at the Cat Scan and the x-rays and said it was Spinal Stenosis. He warned me to not fall, as that could render me paralyzed. He said take it easy. You may get a little bit back, in terms of mobility, but this surgery will stop the continued loss of mobility and annoying symptoms. So I had to wait for a surgery date.

I had felt like I was walking on pillows, I had stabbing pains in my arms and legs, tingling in my arms and legs, headaches, sometimes there was the sensation of cold water running up my leg or arm, Spinal Stenosis is also pain in the leg while walking, and it is also a hard time getting out of a chair to stand up.

The surgery was planned for September 12 the day after my 69th birthday.

I had said to Lorne that I would love to see my favourite group, so I was very fortunate cause Lorne bought tickets for the September 8th Il Divo concert at Rama Casino in Orillia. These 4 guys are such amazing singers. They each have a unique voice, and they are brilliant when they harmonize together. They do easy listening, classical, opera, sung in Italian, Spanish, French...I can't tell you who is my favourite singer in the group? I really couldn't say, they all have something special. Simon Cowell certainly did us ladies a lot of favours by putting these four gents together. It was the best birthday ever!

I had the surgery on a Tuesday, I never had so much pain in my life. The burning, the nerve pain was phenomenal. On Friday they let me go, and I stayed with Cynthia again. She was so good for me, and I was in so much pain, I'd ask her for more pain killers, and it just didn't seem enough to kill that pain. I was a pain in the butt for her. I went home at the end of the month.

Lorne had moved all of our stuff up to the cottage. I went for my check up and all was well, they did a decompression of the vertebrae's C3, C4, C5 and C6 and then he fused them. I am still able to move my head; I have lost about 5% mobility in my neck. It took 18 months for it all to heal. Some of my symptoms were eliminated, the walking and the balance is still pretty bad.

Then not too long ago I complained to my pain specialist about the pain in my lower back and the heaviness in my legs, with pain in my butt. He suggested I have an MRI of my spine, and to organize it through my new family doctor Mara L. Hollingsworth.

Dr. Hollingsworth is a young petite, super intelligent doctor. She is also very nice to talk to, she is a good listener, and she understands how I feel considering that I still have lingering heart issues that are here to stay and anemia of the hemoglobin and B-12 make the tiredness from my heart makes me even more tired.

I also think she called my leg and back ache pseudoclaudication it was all very annoying. This narrowing can be caused by bulging disks, bone spurs or a thickening of the supportive ligaments and arthritis in the back of the spinal canal.

I will meet with a surgeon by telephone on January 13, 2021 at 10:30. Originally Dr. C. Teshima the gastroenterologist said that they will remove the 5 cm polyp in about 2 months. So hopefully COVID won't interfere with the plan. So we will see what happens. I try not to worry.

The other thing that will contribute to the leg pain is more issues with the lower part of my spine. The MRI shows the start of more Stenosis, similar to what I had in my neck. Osteoarthritis, bulging discs and God knows what else. The report has been sent to my pain specialist Dr. Michael Gofeld.

Dr. Gofeld has been instrumental in helping me stay relatively pain free. I will need to make an appointment and see what can be done in addition to my Ketamine Infusions for Fibromyalgia. When a person has suffered from pain a good portion of their life, to be able to get some amazing relief, is such a blessing. I was certainly blessed to be referred to Dr. Gofeld and the Silver Pain Clinic in North York.

Chapter 14:

Bill - August 2018

When we get sick and need to be hospitalized, we are often in very bad shape. We often think that this is reserved for only the elderly.

There are times that we are hospitalized when we just can't be managed at home. During the years that Bill and I were together, it was sometimes difficult to deal with. I believe with diabetics when their blood sugar drops, it is hard to get them to listen, or cooperate. He didn't think that anything needed to be done. When in fact he needed orange juice and a cracker when necessary, but he didn't think it was necessary.

We separated in September of 2010. We felt bad that things hadn't worked out, but I do believe that I had stayed too long looking after a man who wouldn't look after himself.

There were trips to Dairy Queen and drinking alcohol and he went back to smoking. It was like he had a death wish.

He had cellulites so many times I had asked the doctor once how many times could a person recover from cellulites. He was past the number and I would visit him from time to time when he was not well, or when he had had surgery. He had nurses coming in daily. He had gone through 120 days of hyperbaric oxygen chamber treatments for the hole in his foot. Sandra his oldest sister had driven him most of the time from Oshawa to Branson Hospital in Toronto. In the beginning I too had taken him. And in the beginning it seemed like it would be working quite well.

It wasn't too long after his treatments were finished that I met him one day in the waiting room at the doctor's office. I actually walked right past him. We both had doctor appointments. He looked so sick. Bill called me back, and I sat with him for a bit till he got called to see the doctor.

I wish I had asked him if he had his affairs in order? Was he prepared?

He was never the type to be proactive, but I could have guessed that it was something that he would not have thought of.

He called me one day to tell me that the foot he had the hole in, was now having the big toe amputated. Within quite a short period of time he was suffering from more affects of diabetes and infection. He had the foot amputated, and at that point he was admitted to hospital in Bellville. His sisters Sandra and Wanda were making the trip to visit him every week.

The diabetes and the infection in the bone of his leg were quite serious and before I knew about it he had his leg amputated below the knee. Slowly and surely he was being whittled away. And the fact that he wouldn't eat his fruits and vegetables hadn't crossed his mind. He was being transferred to Trenton hospital, and still we didn't know how this was all going to turn out.

I got a call from his sister Sandra and she told me that he had complained about not feeling well.

He was not just suffering with diabetes and amputations, but he had also been diagnosed with cancer. That was also a big blow.

Lorne and I drove down to the farm one Sunday near the end of July. I said, we are 3.5 hours closer to Trenton, I need to go visit Bill, my gut is saying Bill's not doing well.

I drove to Trenton that Sunday afternoon and found him to be sleeping. I sat there for a while and he woke up and he was surprised to see me sitting there. We spoke for a little while and he told me he wasn't doing well. It is really strange to do a chaplaincy call/personal visit to someone you had been married to. He seemed happy that I had come to see him. We had an opportunity to set each other at ease. I was able to say goodbye to him and to forgive him for being such a stubborn man who wouldn't look after himself or me for that matter when we had been a married couple. Bill was a nice guy, a terrible husband, but a great friend. We should never have been married. But...hindsight has 20/20 vision.

I was glad that I had gone to see him, and to be able to say goodbye to him for the last time. He passed away a week later.

The thing is that even when you know that someone is dying, there is still a shock that goes with it. When I heard that Bill had died, it was sadness but also a relief that he was no longer in pain. Because with the illness of diabetes and cancer he did indeed certainly suffer.

Sometimes it is ok to pray for a sick patient to go home. When their suffering is so bad, they really don't want to be here anymore. It is just too painful for them.

We wanted to know if there was going to be a funeral or a get together of some kind of celebration of life. Apparently he didn't want anything.

I found that a little hard to swallow. There were many who wanted to say goodbye. But, his wishes were followed.

Chapter 15:

I Visit the Sick

My ex-husband died August 6, 2018. He died without a Will. No one knew what he wanted. Except to say he didn't want to have a funeral.

When I realized the importance of having the three 'end of life documents' I thought I cannot wait until it is too late. I was covered when I had my open heart surgery when I was still a single woman. But now the situation has changed.

As a chaplain who visited patients in the hospital I often heard what their wishes would be. And if they did speak to me about it, I would suggest that they speak with a family member and organize it so that they would be covered. Either they make a lawyers appointment. And lawyers will come to the hospital to do an appointment, as long as their client is in good mental state.

Since 2011, I have prepared a new Will and Power of Attorney since my situation has changed. My health situation has also changed, and I wanted to be prepared so that my husband would not have to make a decision and feel guilty. I also had assistance from my financial advisor Shirley Mein. She has helped many others put their financial and their end of life paperwork in the form of a Will and Power of Attorney's in order.

0-0-0-0

I want to bring up a subject that we don't often talk about. When we have a friend or a relative who is quite ill, we often hear that they don't want to be having visits with anyone. They will tell their children or friend that they are not in any shape physically to be having people visit them.

The thing is not everyone will understand that decision. But being a loving relative or friend, it is hard to honour that decision. We don't always know what prompts that decision, but we need to understand.

As a bit of background perhaps this explanation will help a bit.

The elderly often need as much care as an infant. Their needs are often looked after in a hospital or nursing home. Because of swallowing issues, their food may need to be specially prepared, or be pureed and made easier to eat so that they don't choke.

The sick and elderly are often bedridden and they need special care so that they don't get bed sores. They need to be repositioned on a regular basis so that their skin does not erupt with sores.

In most cases the patient who is hospitalized perhaps in palliative care, loves a visit from a relative, or a dear friend. But, don't be alarmed if the patient says, no I don't want to see anyone. Try to honour that, although it is often difficult to do.

You of course want to see them, and say goodbye to this friend or relative. The thing is, often because of illness, or surgery or chemo or radiation the patient has a problem talking, or they are so tired and this could also be from medication for pain, they are too weak to have a conversation. They also personally feel they 'look' different, and they subconsciously don't want to be seen without makeup, or in a hospital gown. We are a vain lot you know.

The times I have been in hospital, I always felt I want to still look good, and that way it doesn't worry my family or friend. As a matter of fact, you know how they tell you no nail polish on your fingers or toes. I would actually ask my friend Lynda to come in and put polish on my fingers and toes the day after surgery. I know how vain can you get? And of course that way I would be able to see her as well. But I love her for doing this for me.

If they know someone is going to visit, they want to look good, like they did before they were sick. And really when you think about it, you can't blame them. When Lorne came to visit the day after my open heart surgery he was expecting a train wreck, and because I was feeling ok by the time they brought me to my room from ICU, I put on a little lipstick...and he was relieved that I didn't look like the train had just arrived at my bed. I didn't want him to worry about me.

You go to visit your mom and we say to them, you look fine, just as you are. Do you lie to them to make them feel better? Now lying is not always a good thing. So instead of lying, you could say something like,

'You know mom or George or whoever you are seeing...I am here to see you. The **You** that is my friend, (co-worker, cousin etc) I love you and would do anything for you. I know you are feeling off, and you're in pain, I can see it in your face. I wanted to have a short visit not to pick you apart, but to tell you that I love you.

How you look, doesn't matter to me, I wanted to connect with the person who over the years, we have had so much together, the good times, the bad times. I wanted to visit with the man/woman who has been such a good friend to me. I love you and I needed to tell you that. I wanted to tell you how much I have appreciated you over the years. I wanted to tell you how much fun I have had with you. I want to tell you that I will miss you so much.

After we get released from the hospital, we are sometimes so glad to just be going home we don't care what is going on, we just want to get home.

There were a few things that I had problems with even though I was home, and doing well. I did the cardiac rehab at Lindsay Ross Memorial Hospital near my place, but I never could get the energy back.

I finally went to a voice lesson; I realized that my beautiful soprano voice was now a thing of the past. I still haven't been able to find a new voice that I can identify with or even sing too. But I am reminded it is a small tradeoff to give up singing to actually still *be alive*.

Chapter 16:

Do They Help?

Dying is not a sexy topic. It is something you can't compromise with. You can plan for it, but you never know when or how it will happen.

Even when a patient is terminally ill, when the patient dies from their disease, it is a shock to the family and friends.

So many people treat the topic of death as a taboo subject, and then there are people like myself or Michael Bishop from the Reflections Group, who understand and can easily talk about it. Could it be that since we have both been in life and death situations? Possibly! Or we are just the type that when we were in college or doing our CAPPE Units, we learned to not be afraid of death.

We are familiar with the 5 Stages of Grief identified by Dr. Elizabeth Kubler Ross.

1. Denial: the first stage of grief is Denial. It is really the first of our reactions to any form of sudden loss. We can't believe that the trauma or death has happened. No it couldn't be!
2. Anger: The second stage of grief is Anger, or it could be defined as, I am so angry that you have abandoned me. I am so upset and angry at you for dying.
3. Bargaining: The third stage of grief is Bargaining. You know if I only had

tried a bit harder, or looked better after you, you wouldn't have died. I should not have gone to work that day, if only I had stayed home.
4. Depression: The fourth stage of grief is Depression, I can't get out of bed, I don't want to talk to my friends, and I don't want to go on.
5. Acceptance: The fifth stage of grief is Acceptance. Finally I understand why you had to go. You were in so much pain. I know that you are not in pain anymore. I will always love you.

Every individual experiences loss and grief in their own way and time. The one, who is left to grieve the loss, can go through the various stages in no particular order.

Grief is the price you pay for loving someone. Thank God there is grief, or you never would have realized how much you loved the one you lost.

When we think of the ones we have met in life and how they have reacted to losing someone, you realize we are all different. Some hearts seem to recover quicker than others. There seems to be others that never recover from the death of a loved one.

Ministers are human, and they are fathers, mothers, just like everyone else in society. We do feel loss, and also suffer when we grieve. We also have to work at dealing with our own loses, and not let it affect our professional life.

We are able to understand many of life's situations many of which have been studied in role play while studying. We are prepared to talk about life's problems. Many situations and scenarios are presented when ministry students are studying chaplaincy and counseling in their studies. Also the CAPPE units I studied helped me a great deal when working in a hospital setting.

The experiential studies we do gives us real time experience while studying. The units I studied centered on Intensive Care, Emergency, Mothers and Child Birth, Medical Surgery, Psychiatry, and Cardiac ICU.

We learn to counsel parents of children, and babies, to speak with adult children of elderly patients. If necessary we speak to parents about a baby that was still born, speak with a man who's been asked to take his sick wife with MS off of Life Support. These are all difficult situations for parents, families and spouses.

Speaking to a wife and family about her husband, and father needing palliative care. We have learned to speak with those who are dying and some are wanting. and needing to clear their conscious. We learn to speak with a woman whose husband is abusing her.

We are trained to make suggestions and to pray for those whose lives are drawing to a close. We have been trained to speak to the parents who have just lost a child to suicide. We also need to sometimes deal with a coroner who has to determine if a crime has been committed.

Prior to going back to school in 1999 I was a visiting spiritual care volunteer, visiting members of St. Timothy's at Ajax and Pickering General Hospital or in their home.

Chapter 17:

Pandemic's

In 2020, so many people died and it was attributed to COVID-19 whether it was or not. Many people died and it was reported as a COVID death, yet they themselves didn't have COVID.

Their treatment or tests and surgeries were delayed because of COVID and if they did die, it was listed as COVID in the beginning whether it was or not. Now nine or ten months in, there is talk about going forward and denoting the cause of death more accurately.

I too had tests postponed and I can only imagine if you had something urgent scheduled and it was postponed. Two years ago we talked about ordering an endoscopy and colonoscopy; a year ago I had an appointment to have the consultation done in Parry Sound. After seeing our local gastroenterologist, she sent me to a cardiologist in town who determined that I would be better off to have it done at St. Mikes in Toronto, unless my cardiologist was willing to sign off on it. I didn't think that was a good idea, so I opted to have it done at St. Mikes. My new family doctor was able to secure an appointment for me December 11th 2020. They found a 5 cm polyp which has to be surgically removed. Now, with the second wave of COVID lockdown extended into February, will I have to wait longer a bit longer, until probably May or June.

A 5 cm polyp is large, and I trust that they will be able to remove it in good time, so that it doesn't get the chance to change to a more concerning issue. I trust God that it will all happen in good time. I pray!

The families who lost loved ones during this time are upset and some are downright angry about how this has all happened. Can you blame them? I totally understand.

As I write this, and also the blogs I have written about COVID-19 and the Pandemic, I see a lot of posturing from politicians. I get the distinct feeling that not all the truth is being told to the people.

I know in the beginning, a lot of younger people felt that COVID was all a hoax.

Personally I don't feel it was a hoax. I don't think I am naive. I do feel we are not told the truth about a lot of things. Our own Prime Minister said that he would take this *opportunity* to RESET Canada. Now what does that mean? Would it have something to do with the United Nations Initiative 2030? I think so.

In 2015, 192 counties sign the declaration to unify the world, make it better for all, and there with a number of goals that they wanted to achieve by 2030. That is only 9 years away.

I know over the past centuries many pandemics have attacked this planets people. The following is a list of pandemics or epidemics that you may have heard of over the centuries.

Russian plague: 1770-1772 causes, 100,000 plus deaths!

Philadelphia yellow fever epidemic: in 1793 there were 5,000 deaths!

Flu pandemic: 1889-1890 there were **1,000,000 deaths in 5 weeks!**

In 1916 there was a Polio Epidemic. The polio epidemic started in New York City. There were 27,000 cases and 6,000 deaths in the United States. Children were the victims. And those who survived had permanent disabilities.

It wasn't until 1954 that Salk vaccine was developed. Polio has been greatly reduced but it still isn't eradicated. It took 38 years to get a vaccine.

Spanish Flu: 1918-1920

The Spanish flu, also known as the 1918 flu pandemic, was an unusually deadly influenza pandemic caused by the H1N1 influenza A virus. Lasting from February 1918 to April 1920, it infected 500 million people – about a third of the world's population at the time – in four successive waves. (During WW1)

Asian Flu: 1957-1958

The Asian Flu pandemic was another global showing for influenza. With its roots in China, the disease claimed more than 1 million lives.

AIDS pandemic and epidemic: 1981-present day has caused **35 million deaths.** Now, about 64% of the estimated 40 million living with human immunodeficiency virus (HIV) live in sub-Saharan Africa.

H1N1 Swine Flu pandemic: 2009-2010. The 2009 swine flu pandemic was caused by a new strain of H1N1 that originated in Mexico in the spring of 2009 before spreading to the rest of the world. In one year, the virus infected as many as 1.4 billion people across the globe and killed between 151,700 and 575,400 people, according to the CDC.

West African Ebola epidemic: 2014-2016 has 28,600 reported cases and 11,325 deaths.

Zika Virus epidemic: 2015-present day. Zika is usually not harmful to adults or children, it can attack infants who are still in the womb and cause birth defects. It may be a few years before the total affect can be determined.

SARS Severe Acute Respiratory Syndrome in 2003. We think of SARS as a pandemic, yet they said there were not enough cases to be a considered a pandemic.

Respiratory disease caused by corona virus infection. It sure did scare people. It was considered extremely rare (Fewer than 100 cases per year in Canada)

Chapter 18:

It Keeps Coming

I believe that with this COVID-19 that the world is taking a more proactive stance. If we look at a map and see the hot spots, you would never want to leave home.

The population of the earth steadily gets a little larger and before you know it we have over 7.7 Billion people on the planet.

That is a lot of people. Most have families. And they all at one time had someone to love them and help them, mother and look after them with tender loving care.

And the sweet thing about the departure and the arrival...the souls are all loving. The birth and the death is actually a very lonely process, especially during COVID.

And if they are able ...perhaps a hug, or hold their hand and just talk like you did when there was nothing wrong with either one of you, like the old days.

0-0-0-0

A visit with a sick relative can be draining. If you have to do most of the talking, it can be very tiring. Like, what do we talk about now?

You bring a little something; don't be disappointed if they are not too thrilled with your gift.

Don't be disappointed if they don't offer you a chocolate from that box of chocolate they just brought you.

Don't be shocked if they ask you to paint their toes nails. I knew someone like that. Oh it was me. After surgery I always asked Lynda, my little sis to paint my toe nails. I'd make sure my legs were shaved before surgery, and when Lynda came to visit, I had the polish ready, the emery board and the polish remover there (in case of a little slip) Oh we are still vain when we are sick or uncomfortable after surgery.

We the patient is not concerned with your comfort, they are glad you are there, but they wouldn't mind having a sleep, and if you wanted to stay that is ok. Cause they will be feeling a lot better after a nap.

Things are different in 2020! The year of COVID-19! How will we ever forget this year? This is also the year that many seniors died in Long Term Care Facilities.

This is the year that many chose to ignore what was suggested by those in authority in many countries. And these were not 3rd world countries...The United States of America was probably the last to come on board and take COVID seriously.

Their President Donald Trump in my estimation did not take COVID seriously in the beginning; hence the red dot's completely cover the map of the USA.

Travel is halted to unnecessary driving across the shared Canadian and American borders. And I do believe that it's a good thing. But you can still fly across the border into the USA and back. The sooner people stay home, the sooner this virus will die out as well. COVID needs us to transport itself to a new host /person in new places so that it can attack unnoticed and make more people ill and the virus is active and surviving and now mutating. The people keep on moving (commuting) from town to town. As this is being written, France, The UK and the Netherlands are locked down, as I am sure European countries in lockdown.

Total lockdown implemented to stop the virus in its tracks...I hope it to be a positive initiative, and I honestly believe that it will make a difference in the flattening of the COVID curve.

People, we need to stay home, so that this virus dies. We have been asked to do this from the beginning. But some choose not to listen, because some omnipotent people totally believe that the COVID virus is a hoax. Now I do believe that some of the COVID virus information we have been told is an out and out exaggeration of the facts.

This is not a hoax my friends! When a family member has passed away because of

COVID directly or because of lack of treatment or delay due to COVID, it hurts very much to be saying that it is a hoax.

The other thing that I am very disappointed in, how our Prime Minister, Justin Trudeau is using the opportunity of COVID to **'Reset'** our country. To reset something is like resetting the stove clock...you put it back to the accurate time. But Justin Trudeau has something quite different in mind. And I am hoping that his Reset will be called a Hoax as well.

I'm having a hard time trusting our Prime Minister. He has broken laws and should be brought up on charges...and dealt with like any other person who would have done something similar. He never answers a question with a straight answer. He gives a slick answer too without saying a thing. When his lips move...I do not trust what he says, one bit...Remember, his transparent office promise? His office is Teflon lined and all the crap that happens in there just slides down the walls, and he shovels it out, and feeds us the slippery lies...his sneaky antics of slipping information into a budget **The SNC-Lavalin** affair was a political scandal involving attempted political interference with the justice system by the Prime Minister of Canada, Justin Trudeau. The charges allege that between 2001 and 2011, SNC-Lavalin paid CA$48 million in bribes in Libya to officials in the government of Muammar Gaddafi. They also allege that at the same time, the company defrauded Libyan organizations of CA$130 million.

And what about the WE Scandal? Well this isn't the book for all the bull that is hanging around on Parliament Hill. But, the information above is an accurate portrayal of what the Canadian PM is associated with, and involved with, the SNC-Lavalin is only one company. How many other companies are out there who are pulling the same antics? And it all gets covered up.

Getting back to COVID and how the population in Canada is being treated and fed misinformation. The people that are creating the fear of COVID are also selling us the vaccine. That to me is a huge conflict of interest.

The vaccine approval has been fast tracked. But they forget to tell us that the ferrets that were given the vaccine in the trials all died. Ferrets were used because their immune system is very similar to ours. Are we the test for this vaccine? Anything that is not tested properly should not be given to the public. We do not know what will happen? (Perhaps the Prime Minister and his cronies should get it first?)

The United Nations goal is to lower the planets population to 270,000,000 for a sustainable future on the planet...the vaccine seems like a nice way to start achieving that goal although I am sure that 2030 is not the goal date for that. I am not just spouting out a piece of false news here.

This United Nations Initiative has Canada and about 191 other countries signed on to this goal/plan for the year 2030. The initiative is full of 'pie in the sky' suggestions for a better future, their words, not mine.

It is a 'new but old way' of living that the Russians discarded years ago because it didn't work. But they are calling it socialism this time.

And the same big dollar investors in the COVID vaccine like Bill Gates stand to get richer and richer and richer...Bill Gates, I remind you, you can't take it with you! If you have billions, why do you need more? What is good for the goose is good for the gander isn't it? So the rich get richer under the UN initiative and the middle class disappears into the slums or maybe into oblivion? And who gets left behind…. to make up the 270,000,000? The rich elite? They will want a pristine planet, and since you can't buy a new one, the planet as it is now is in total disrepair…so let's clean it up for the money men…let's not forget that their factories and jets contribute greatly to the disrepair of the planet.

All I do know for sure is that the rich have their shit together! They have their finances in order, they have their POA's in order and they have a valid Last Will and Testament in order. They wouldn't for a minute leave their estates unprotected so that the government can take hold of it.

They are in fact the controlling factor behind the government.

So if we can't be rich, we can have our affairs in order and leave the planet to *our* heirs.

0-0-0-0

The Pharmaceutical industry has made a killing over the years because there is no accountability. They won't be held responsible if the vaccine does something terrible to your body, your nervous system, or other organs.

Think of all the children with autism...1 in 66 according to the Public Health Agency of Canada...Yet I have heard 1 in 45 but then as I was reading about autism, it was very clear that it said, that the cause was NOT vaccinations. The other thing is the correlation of the onset of vaccinations and the rise in the occurrence of autism runs pretty well parallel.

One in 66 Canadian children is diagnosed with the neurological condition, the Public

Health Agency of Canada reported in 2018, and according to Autism Ontario about 100,000 people in Ontario, including **40,000** children, are on the autism spectrum. (As of Mar 15, 2019)

Well, you are reading this, and you are probably wondering what do I believe? And my answer is, who do you want to believe today? I imagine it is all a little bit true, depending who spins it.

I heard and saw a report https://youtu.be/ZaV7m2S4KXA on YouTube about the aluminum content in the COVID vaccine. We have all heard in the past the aluminum causes Alzheimer's. We have all heard before that there are chemicals and aluminum in vaccines. These are not healthy ingredients for a growing body, or an aging body.

For those who were around in the 60's you may remember the aftermath of

Thalidomide, and if I'm not mistaken, Thalidomide was rushed through the testing and approval process and caused horrific deformities and missing limbs in new born infants. I would hate to see a new vaccine do the same or something just as significant. Fast tracking without proper testing does not constitute good and responsible medicine as far as I am concerned.

DÉJÀ VU the 60's Thalidomide!

I was advised to take the COVID vaccine, because I am high risk. It also has Bill Gates written all over it. And I do not trust Bill Gates. But I do trust my doctor.

If we all sucked in our gut, and said, you know, the only way we can stop COVID is to stop commuting...stop driving here and there. The way I think is this...we take the bull by the horns and say, enough is enough. We stop travelling, and we wait it out. STAY HOME!

And then on Boxing Day we all went into a Lockdown, in the effort to flatten the curve of the Pandemic here in this province.

Yet many were still able to fly in and out of the USA or to other international destinations. And they say the border is closed. So as long as this continues it could be a while before the spread of COVID is stopped.

For people living in apartment buildings this must be very tough living. Waiting for elevators that are empty! Doing laundry could become difficult, for those who have to use a public laundry room. Going shopping may be impossible for you. You may end up ordering groceries, and carefully following the COVID rules pick them up at the curb at the grocery store.

0-0-0-0

At this point COVID has been around since March of 2020, and people are getting tired of waiting, weary of having to put up with the inconvenience and the uncertainty of the unseen! Some just don't care anymore. Some people are so lonesome, they don't care anymore. I say, hang in there, there has to be a light at the end of the tunnel that isn't a train, but a ray of sunshine to make your life better again. But in the mean time, because of the spread of the virus, and the untimely deaths of so many during these last months, it is imperative, that we all get our things in order. I am not making this into scare tactics, but I am being realistic, when our friends and relatives are not able to come and go to where ever we want, it means that we are not free to do as we like. It also means we have to be prepared.

I realize there are those who say it is a hoax. Tell that to the son or daughter or the spouse who is left behind. This is a real virus that is killing people!

I have spoken to people who have survived COVID. It is a horrible illness that that doesn't discriminate and it not only takes the elderly and the ones with underlying illnesses, it kills the young as well. The Second Wave is here, and the numbers are much higher than before (8 months ago), Ontario Premier Doug Ford, announced on Thursday, December 17th over 2432 new cases in Ontario. The cases keep rising.

Read through the 7 day average number of + cases, is about 3400 on January 8th 2021.

We are living in times were fear grapples people who are perhaps immune compromised, or over the age of 65, diabetic, heart and lung issues and many other health issues.

If everyone were to take this more seriously I think that we could see the numbers come down and flatten as they say. But many more city folk are going to have to start seeing how careless behaviour in the hot spots of the countries is not prudent to getting this virus under control.

Those with Chronic ailments, Diabetes, Heart and Lung conditions, Fibromyalgia, and many other ailments make you a target. Those who are senior citizen, particularly over the age of 65 are at risk.

Wash your hands frequently, use sanitizers on your hands, the handle of a grocery card, door knobs etc. Wear a mask in stores, public buildings. Stay within your family bubble.

If you are elderly, ask a younger person for help, picking up groceries. Have them delivered to your front door.

COVID was the virus that seemed to be attracted to seniors particularly 65 and over. Those with diabetes; and other auto-immune diseases are also at risk of catching the virus.

Those with heart and lung issues are also high risk and if you have any of these conditions, you need to be careful to not be in public places, or taking any risks.

The lockdowns in Ontario started in mid March and Lorne would go out once a week to get groceries and pick up meds for me. During the lockdown pharmacies are only giving 30 days worth of prescription drugs. We have to remain on top of it, or we run out...as we get a little older, this is sometimes hard to figure out...so we do our best.

What I usually suggest to people when they start to age; is to speak to their pharmacist and have them do a bubble pack for their elderly patients. That way there is no confusion, and people are able to take their meds without worry or guessing.

We heard of friends who have parents in the hospital, and it breaks my heart to hear that they can't go to visit their mother or father. The only thing that they were able to do was speak to them on Skype or Zoom if they were lucky. These are the worst days for some people. They can't speak to their loved ones who are on pieces of equipment like ventilators, their family members die and because they haven't been in a situation like this before, or they don't want to speak about death, those who are left behind to make arrangements, don't have any idea what to do, because their loved one never said what it was that they wanted at end of life. It has all happened so quickly.

The thing is we don't plan funerals and celebrations of life every day unless you are a funeral director, or you are a minister who does funerals as part of his/her church activities. The average person is not a funeral expert.

With each service I have learn a little more. You definitely know what you don't want.

I also have learned that it is ok to show some emotion when you are speaking with your family. You need to be able to say, look guys, one of these days, I am going to die. I know you don't like talking about it. But it is important to me that I help you plan it out, so that you will know what I want, we can do it together.

Perhaps we can all talk about it and we can all make plans for our end of life ceremony. (See the Appendix 3 at the back of the Book)

My goodness friends, these sure are scary times for some people within our circle of friends or communities during COVID-19. We are isolated from our neighbours, families and friends. The only contact is by telephone, SKYPE, Face-Time, Facebook, or yelling across the yard. All because we have been told to Safe Distance at least 2 meters and Self Isolate and Stay at Home until we are declared safe to go out again.

For Lorne and I, it isn't too bad. We are by ourselves, fortunately we like each other so it isn't a stressful process, as it is for some. I always said, if I had to be locked up with someone, I am glad it is him. For those who know me personally you will understand what I mean.

I have personally heard of numerous situations whereby the family is restricted from visiting critically ill patients. It isn't just the coronavirus COVID-19 that people are sick with and dying from, there is all the regular illness and household accidents, heart attacks, strokes and treatments for cancer for example that continue. Patients are feeling isolated because they are, and their family and friends are feeling helpless, because they can't interact and physically visit to be with them.

Your loved one is being looked after by a front line worker who works for a hospital or home nursing company. And unless you are isolated with the patient in a facility, you cannot see them in most cases, nor can you monitor what is going on there. I feel if you have a mom or a dad in a nursing facility, with the bad press some of these places were given during the first wave in Ontario, anyone with a parent there is probably holding their breath at the moment.

It is a very vulnerable position that these elderly people are in. I feel so helpless. I have a few friends who are in a nursing or retirement home. They are I call it being held hostage. You can't take them out for a visit or shopping at the moment. You can't eat with them, which is usually a fond past time. Some visit only once a week and it's for a short period of time after a negative COVID test.

Some hospitals have set up visiting for only one other person as the family delegate. And it's the ritual of gowning up in isolation gear. The gown, gloves, mask, booties, face shield and hair covering, it must be frightening for the patient to wonder who is behind all that cover up. But we are grateful if they are able to provide that for us.

In most cases, it is better to arrange a phone call with the patient's give yourself a little bit of time so that you can prepare what you would like to say. You have to be prepared for a one sided conversation if your loved one is on a ventilator, or is sedated.

If they can't hold the phone, have the nurse put the phone on speaker and lay it on their bed near their head, adjust the volume so as not to frighten the patient or disturb others in the same room. Be gentle and respectful and not too loud as you speak to your loved one. It's not a time for settling a score, or telling them negative stuff, it is a time to tell them you love them.

People often wonder if a patient can hear you. Yes, they can hear you.

They maybe aren't able to speak, and if that is the case, you do all the talking.
Speak clearly and succinctly, you should maybe write out a few points that you can speak to him/her about. Such as fond memories, remember when's, a wedding or a special birthday. Tell them how you felt, what you like about. Let them know how you feel.

When the patient is a mom, grandma or 'oma', (that is what my grandchildren call me,) this is what I would want to hear from them, in my final days or hours; that they LOVE me, and that they are thinking of me. All the rest would be secondary.

You have heard the statement, "You can't take it with you." Well that is true of material things, your money, stocks and bonds, your jewels, your house and belongings. But what you can take with you is the Love that you have been shown throughout the course of your life. The love you have given and the love you have received.

So when you tell grandma or grandpa that you love her/him, it is the one and only thing (with it's that warm feeling of love) that can go with them when they pass away.

I grant you Courage, Strength and Wisdom as you go through the process of saying goodbye. It is never easy. And it is possible that there will be tears shed. It's an emotional time. Now, if you believe that you will meet again sometime when you are both not on the planet anymore, there is joy in knowing you will be reunited in the afterlife.

My next thought is sadder in that when they die, the funeral has to be delayed until the COVID-19 isolation is over. But that does not need to be a negative. It gives you time to adjust, and prepare a nice send off.

It could be a couple of months before you can actually celebrate grandma or grandpa's life together as a family and or with friends. But it doesn't have to be a sad time. Some of the best Celebration of Life, that I have attended, included lots of stories and humour. You can plan to celebrate their life instead of having a somber funeral. Now a day, we tend to go more towards the celebration of life.

Thank God we are never privy to when one is going to die, but there is comfort in knowing that we can celebrate a special life with love and joy, respect and laughter, I know when I go, I want you to know that I will take your love with me and it will sustain me for eternity. I wouldn't want you to mourn me. I would want you to honour me by sharing great stories about us, mixed in with laughter, reminisce the good, with the bad, and share with my friends and family what we did, etc. Show them that I was a fun person and not always so serious and stuffy as we ministers are known to be. And I would want them to know that I loved my family, didn't see enough of them. And that I did have my s#*t together.

Chapter 19:

Thank You Charlotte

We don't watch regular network television, here in Dunchurch we are on satellite delivery, so we watch series of programs…a great way to watch! No commercials, no repetitive news.

One of the series that we really enjoy is called Alaska the Last Frontier. It is about the Kilcher family and how they are self sufficient, and homestead. The original Kilcher came from Switzerland and settled in Alaska: The Last Frontier focuses on the

Kilcher family. The Kilchers comprise the patriarch Atz Kilcher, whose parents were natives of Switzerland and had moved to Alaska way back during the reign of Adolf Hitler. Otto Kilcher is the family rancher married to Charlotte Kilcher as his wife. Eivin is Otto and Charlotte's son.

The other members of the family include Atz Lee, Atz's son, and Jane, Atz Lee's wife. Eve is Eivin's wife.

The Last Frontier chronicles the life of four generations of the Kilcher clan who reside in a homestead located outside Homer in Alaska. Their land spans across 640 acres and for miles, there's nothing but wilderness. They survive by being resourceful, and using all what nature offers on health care provider.

Without basic amenities such as running water, they must "hunt, garden, gather, raise and protect livestock, cleverly recycle old-as-new and rely on their innovation in order to survive Alaska's uncontrollable elements. Always pushed to their limits, the Kilchers both work together as a family and face conflicts between old and young generations" — as described by Discovery.

Season 9 continues to document this journey and focuses on the Kilchers as they tackle some serious personal issues as well. While Atz Lee and Jane Kilcher's marriage is at a crossroads they say, Kelli is diagnosed with Multiple Sclerosis. Even Eiven and Eve Kilcher and Otto and Charlotte Kilcher are facing problems in their relationships. The latest season should pick up the story from here while following the Kilcher family as they survive in the harsh Alaskan wilderness by sticking together — amidst all the differences. If there are problems you wouldn't know it.

We enjoy watching the series. The interactions of Otto and his wife Charlotte are lovely. The family is very innovative.

Atz's daughter is Jewel the recording artist. She sings the opening credits/intro with her dad Atz.

Due to COVID Charlotte had noticed that there are very few orders for her beautiful peonies. She grows a huge patch of gorgeous peonies, and ships them to various venues for weddings. This year very fewer brides had ordered peonies because of the COVID restrictions for gatherings.

So Charlotte wanted to do something meaningful for the victims of COVID. She thought about it and she decided to float hundreds of flowers in the bay in memory of those who have died due to COVID.

(photo: Charlotte Kilcher floated hundreds of peonies for those who died of COVID-19 in 2020)

The tribute show was on December 11, 2020, I happened to watch it the following day. Charlotte wrote, "Photos from July of our flower tribute to honor those who have died of COVID-19. This was shown on last Sunday's episode of Alaska the Last Frontier on Discovery. My heart goes out to all of you who are suffering now and to all of those who have died. Sending love and flowers out to the world. From my family to you and yours. Alaska Beauty Peony Co-op"

Honour the Dead, They Deserve to be Celebrated

Yes of course the death of a loved one is traumatic, but it is important that these dear people be celebrated and honoured, so that there can be wonderful stories told, and you actually come away from a funeral feeling ok, you had perhaps even learned something about the deceased that you didn't know. When the fellowship or reception is held at the end of a service… you would have something to talk about with the other guests and family that were present.

(photo: Charlotte Kilcher with help from her family after they set hundreds of peonies afloat in the bay.)

Chapter 20:

It's ok to be angry.
I was a sickly child, and my teenage years were no better. And now 60 years later…it's no different, I'm still sick all the time.

A year ago I was doing pulpit supply in Magnetawan. While doing the service I found myself running out of breath. And the dance started again similar to what I had in 2015. Tired, no energy…and I had all the tests over again…This time not so lucky!

Ticked off, Upset, Very Sad, Disappointed! Worried!

I am writing this because I was given the announcement by my heart surgeon Dr. David Latter, a mitral valve specialist at St. Michaels Hospital in Toronto on the 24th January, 2020, that I cannot have my repaired heart, fixed again or my mitral valve replaced. "There is nothing to suture a new mitral valve to. There is too much calcium around the valve and there is some blockage within the valve."

If he were to sew into the calcium, it could and probably would crumble like the shell of an egg.

This surgeon told me that he always asks himself, "Will this be a good outcome for the patient?" If the answer is 'No' he doesn't operate. He told me, there is a very good chance that I would not come off of the operating room table. The surgery would be much too risky. At least he was honest in his opinion and I appreciated that.

In 2015 his attitude and demeanor had been so much livelier, positive and he had a very dramatic way of telling me he was the best, and he is the best for this type of surgery. Plus you need to have that arrogance if you are going to be putting your hands on a person's heart. You don't want to hear, "well, hopefully we'll get in there and fix you up. Your chances of survival is pretty good, see you tomorrow." I wouldn't want him for a doctor.

During the month of December of 2019, I had numerous heart related tests including a transesophageal ultra sound, echo cardiogram and an angiograph.

The day I received my diagnosis and prognosis, I initially felt so helpless, and disappointed. What was I to do? First I was stunned; I could barely speak to ask a question. My throat was dry, my mouth and tongue was thick, and I could barely open my mouth. I had heard enough. We left the hospital that afternoon and it was very quiet in the car. We drove to Oshawa to visit our good friend Douggie Baird, my Chair of Session from Scugog Island United Church, in Port Perry.

Douggie was a strong man, a man of principle a loving husband, who always protected and looked after his wife, his church, job and his friends, the man with the gravelly voice, who loved to read scripture.

I met Douggie and Susie through Michael Bishop, and for a number of years while Michael and I did pulpit supply for Douggie's church we developed a lovely working relationship but also a good friendship. He would often say" Between Bishop Bowers and Baird we get it done." Douggie was a deeply spiritual man, who knew his scripture lessons, and loved to be in the pulpit. If he had had a second chance at another career, I am sure he would have been a very popular and meaningful minister.

I'll never forget the Sunday morning he rode up on large horse dressed as John Wesley, carrying his big book, ready to do one of his 'Wesley' sermons.

I told him one day about my father, and how he used to phone me from the Netherlands and if he had his accordion he would play, Stevie Wonder's, "I Just Called to Say I Love You." I had told Douggie how much I had missed him. He told me that he missed his dad too. You see he could relate, he had lost his father much too soon, and he never got over it. So after that, whenever he called he would say or sing to me, I just called to say I love you. And he would chuckle and we would chat, and he'd always say, if you want me to read scripture I'm available.

Douggie had a battle with throat cancer. He had surgery in Toronto. His body had betrayed him too. He was doing well in the beginning, considering that he now was unable to speak. He had been home for a number of months recuperating. But during that time, he was growing frustrated. Communicating was difficult and increasingly more frustrating. He was told that radiation would have been used as well in case there were any malignant cells left in his body. He would have to go to Toronto every day. He couldn't see himself travelling to Toronto everyday in winter weather, and he said no. He also refused the other surgery that would have given him an artificial larynx. He knew what he was willing to take and do, but some of this he couldn't do. He wasn't willing to compromise.

But now he was hospitalized in Oshawa at Lakeridge Health in palliative care. He couldn't speak anymore. In his own way he had given up. If he couldn't speak anymore to his beloved Susie, or read scripture, or call his kitty cat Shadow, he wanted to leave this world on his own terms and be reunited with his Mom and Dad. He was stubborn and liked to do it his way.

When that booming voice didn't work for him anymore he decided that 'Half a Rev' (that is how he referred to himself as,) had had enough.

The other thing was that he had been friends and had a great respect for Rev. Fraser Lacey. Rev Lacey had passed away in the previous year, and Douggie had lost a great friend and spiritual mentor.

On the 24th of January 2020, we stopped to visit Douggie on our way home. I had received my bad news. I needed to see my friend Douggie. I didn't plan on telling him my news. But I did want to talk to him about our friendship, and that we loved him and Susie.

I hadn't seen Douggie for a while, because for a few months he had told Susie he didn't want to see anyone, even the people who loved him. I could understand this, because of the communication issue, and he probably thought how awkward it would be. But later he let us in.

Michael went to visit, and spent time with him and Susie. His friend Steve Ciecwierc who came from Poland to bid farewell his good friend Douggie; and spend time with Susie, it was good for all concerned. Knowing Michael from his chaplaincy days at the Oshawa hospital I knew that he would be able to bring comfort to Douggie.

The other thing is that when one has a spouse in palliative care, and they don't want to see anyone come to visit, it puts a heavy load on the spouse. In a way, it puts too much responsibility on the spouse in my estimation. You need to see and have support from your friends. We want to be everything we can be to a sick husband. Unfortunately you run out of energy. You run out of ideas. You run out of time.

You see, when you are in the process of losing your spouse, you too need friendship, and support. So I was so pleased to hear that he was finally seeing his friends.

There were many dear friends who wanted to tell Douggie that they loved him, and that they too would keep in touch with his beautiful Susie.

I spoke to him in a way that he could answer yes or no by nodding or giving thumbs up or down. We talked about our friendship, and his church on the island. Also about the good and meaningful things I would remember about him. I spoke to him about happiness in his life and was he afraid of anything. Was he angry that his body had betrayed him? I believe so. And that I could understand very well.

I told him that often when people get sick, their bodies change, they are disappointed that things aren't the same. We lose parts of ourselves; that we felt help define us, and we get angry, because we are sick, get old, we get tired and we know that life as we knew it is changing. We blame God and we are angry! Quite often people, who have had a very strong belief system in place, feel let down by God.

Douggie and I talked about that, and I told him, that often God gets a lot of flak from those whose body has let them down. And I reminded him that God has big shoulders and wouldn't hold it against him. God understands these things because he is God. But, I also reminded Douggie how God had suffered for us without anger. And that tired face smiled and he let me know that all would be good, he was a strong man of faith and conviction and I don't believe he went to meet his Lord with anger in his heart. I think that all was forgiven by then.

I told him I understood, (especially after my appointment earlier that afternoon) I held his hand, and I didn't tell him my story of woe. I could see he was tired. I told him we were leaving for Dunchurch soon. Lorne arrived back in the room time to bid farewell to our friend and we were off. We knew it would be the last time we had seen our friend.

I was weary too it had been a long day, and my news hadn't been that uplifting for me. I needed to get home. Yes I was tired. I needed to talk to myself the way I had spoken to Douggie.

Douggie died the following week. We knew it was going to happen, yet it was still a shock when we heard. I was so grateful that we had still been able to see him and that we had still been able to communicate.

His Celebration of Life was held shortly before the COVID lockdown in Ontario. I was honoured to be able to speak at his Celebration of life. When Lorne and I arrived at Scugog Island United Church, we were asked to sit in the first pew because I was a speaker. I looked at the bulletin and I noticed that I was the first speaker. Put the pressure on, but I was so pleased to be able to honour Douggie and share his humour and love with them.

Scugog Island United Church, *the little church with the big heart*, was packed with family and friends. I had spoken to Susie, Douggie's wife about what she wanted me to speak about. How about something that has humour in it... It wasn't difficult to find things to talk about. This is what I said...

 I am honoured to be able to speak today and to share a few things about our friend and my chair of session Douglas Wesley Baird.

I meet Douggie and Susie Baird in 2011 when I was doing Pulpit Supply here at Scugog Island United church along with Michael Bishop, Douggie called us the

<u>"The 3 B's" Bishop, Bowers, & Baird</u>. He would religiously change the front church sign to reflect who was coming to do pulpit supply and what the message was going to be...that week.

We hit it off immediately. He'd call me up to talk to me about what my service would be about, and to let me know that <u>he was available to read scripture</u>.

Douggie would <u>always call prior to his services at the Retirement</u> and Nursing homes in Port Perry. He would tell how Marilyn DiPoalo and Steve Ciecwierz would go with him to play the music, and how they enjoyed the music,...then he'd say, I think I'll do the story of the Good Samaritan...I said "Douggie, isn't it getting a little stale?" No, he would say, in the nursing home they sleep right through the service.   But if you think they need something new I'll do something new.

He was quite young when his father had died and he felt cheated. He never got over it. He often spoke of his dad. I shared with him that when my dad lived in Europe, my dad would call playing, Stevie Wonder's, "I Just Called to Say I Love You" on his accordion. We both missed our fathers.

So Douggie after that would at least 3 or 4 times a week call...Hi Rev, ½ a Rev here, "I just called to say I love you." And if Susie was away, I think he would miss her, he'd call more often.

He was a serious lay minister. And he loved to talk about John Wesley his preacher hero. I remember Douggie arriving on horseback for his outdoor Wesley Service. He enjoyed being in character. Someone had lent him a horse and Douggie dressed as John Wesley came walking into the church yard, long coat, and hat, bible under his arm, on top of a mighty horse. We were incredulous.

He also enjoyed being in the pulpit, and like most ministers, he enjoyed--- believe it or not...<u>interments and funeral</u>s. He'd say, You know rev, I was honored to do so and so's internment<u>. I made it personal. They would have liked it</u>.

When I was in the pulpit I often asked him to read scripture for me.

He always loved doing anything within the service.

This one particular Sunday about 3 years ago, I had asked him to read for me.. I had invited Douggie up to read Scripture and I sat down.

As he walks up it was always Hello Rev.

I was sitting in the chair while he was organizing his Good News Bible and his papers at the pulpit. And he was taking his time….shuffling things, I was wondering if maybe he had forgotten something? Or did he need help? So under my breath…I said, "Douggie, Have you got your shit together?" He turned around and said, "I do, I do Rev."

Well 3 months later, he called one day and he said…do you remember what you said to me that day in church? No what did I say…I say a lot.

He chuckled and he said, don't you remember? You asked me if I had my shit together...You know that was priceless. I loved it that you asked me that.

You know when he got sick and went to hospital, things got a little more quiet round our place.

You were such a good hearted soul, and Scugog Islands Best Diplomat. For a man to lose his voice when the voice was so authoritative and descriptive must have been so hard for him.

Judging by the turn out today, He would be so happy to know that he had made such an impression on so many people. He would have liked this very much.

You know Douggie, Lorne and I sure do miss your calls ...Rest in Peace dear friend.

Chapter 21:

Run for the hills

You remind yourself, don't run, you're too tired.

I didn't see this coming! I knew I was feeling off, but I certainly didn't think it was this bad.

I realize not that I am not invincible, or that I have some special power to just keep on going forever like the Energizer Bunny, although I have made a good attempt.

I saw that I was not invincible. I felt totally hopeless, and on the way home from the hospital I felt betrayed by my body.

Let down by my repaired mitral valve! But you know that that isn't quite true...It's the calcium girl! Too much damned calcium!

I felt betrayed and disappointed because they didn't give me the all the information I really wanted to know, or the years I thought I would have left. In all fairness, this doctor couldn't answer these questions. I think God would have a better idea.

You see, this will eventually kill me. I will only be able to go on for so long with a heart that has trouble beating; a valve that is clogging up with calcium. Although I am told I won't have a heart attack...I will start slowing down more than what I have already.

Because I think young in my head, I keep forgetting that I too am getting a day older. I don't notice it so much when I look in the mirror. I know, we all choose to ignore some of the truths that are right in front of us.

Because of the blockage, and the calcium that is building up, I am living on borrowed time. One day I probably won't wake up. Now knowing this makes my resolve even more crucial.

I feel I need to be prepared for what lies ahead, and do it with grace, and make it so that my family doesn't suffer any additional pain.

Now I am no different than any other person on the planet. We are all born. The moment we are born, we start to die a little. The hope is always that we grow old first. That we have a nice long life, do the things we want and need to do, as well as accomplish all that we want to achieve. Live a life that we can be happy with, and be at ease and at peace.

In church I had asked Douggie if he had his s#*t together. And because of having asked that of my friend, I knew that I also had to ask myself that question. Knowing Douggie, he did indeed have it together. He had left his affairs in order, so that Susie could go forward without extra worries. So that was an honorable thing to do.

But many people are still afraid to speak of making plans for the future when one of you will pass away.

We all will die on day. Not one of us is immortal! We may like to think we are, we are all in the same boat.

Chapter 22:

Live In Peace

When someone dies, we say Rest in Peace so and so why don't we 'Live in Peace,' before we Rest in Peace?

Well I am here to tell you that as you are living your life with everyday chaos and distractions mixed in with wonderful moments, and challenges, you should also **live** your life in Peace.

How is That Possible to Live in Peace?

When you think of Peace...it reminds me of

calm and beautiful meadows, perhaps with sheep on it, wandering the land. A quiet pastoral scene; not necessarily a religious scene, because we are not all religious. This is being written for all to ponder.

In my picture of Live in Peace, I would have love, respect, forgiveness and happiness present.

I would surround myself with the people who love me and care about me. These same people would also respect me, and it would be a mutual thing were by I would also love and respect them.

If we had ever disappointed each other, I would hope that we would apologize and forgive each other, so that none of us would be laying awake at night wondering if the other was upset with me, angry, or disappointed in me. We would communicate and talk it out, so that we would know for certain that all was well.

Live with Love. Do you remember seeing the love of your life that very first time? Yes! If you are a mother or father, of course you remember laying your eyes on that beautiful child you brought home from the hospital. How did you feel? Didn't your heart just melt?

Towards the last third of your life, you have accumulated many special people in your life, and also many things.

There are those who are family... your children, the grandchild that you love so much, the children of friends. And of course your friends. Surround yourself with people that love you and you love them as well. Surround yourself with people who make you smile and laugh. You know what they say, 'laughter is the best medicine.'

It is also good to have some younger friends, because there are going to be times in life that you need someone younger than yourself to help you with a specific thing. Something you can't do yourself anymore, or you can't ask that older friend to help…it wouldn't feel right to do that. So always have a few whippersnappers in your arsenal of golden goodies. I would be making a new will. (see appendix for making a will.)

Live with Respect. Yes, that's right, life with fun in your life but also live with respect. If you are an older grandma, look the part; leave the miniskirts of the 70's behind for the younger ones. No one wants to see the veins in your legs, or heaven forbid you bend over to pick up something or pet a dog.

Our parents always said, 'make sure you don't embarrass me!' You know what I mean. It is ok to be silly, but do that in private and not with your grandchildren when you're out in public. You know what kids are like, they get so easily shocked by what old people do. And if they only knew that they themselves were like when they were little. And if you think hard, you too will remember how Granny always said something that would turn your cheeks red.

Save the silly, joking things for when your friend Trish is there, and you play with each other's new hair style...and decide that the sides shouldn't be even and you take a good clip off the side at the bottom, you comb the back of your hair in place and decide you should have done this 30 years sooner. For the men, it is the same, different hair cut or shave it all off. Joke with your buddies, and have fun with your grandsons, but be careful you don't embarrass them, lol of course we won't!

You don't live 40, 60, 80 or 100 years and not know what is expected. Ha, they think I am getting old and that I really don't know anything. They think I am just a useless old lady know, but really I have a lot of knowledge and wisdom, if they would only ask? After I am gone, it is too late to ask.

Now about 6 years ago, I made a video for my family and friends, and I also wrote a book about my family. Where did all you kids come from. What was your heritage, your background? Who's who of our family. I was so happy to have made that for the kids and nieces and nephew, because a short 4 weeks after Christmas, my mitral valve blew. I thought for sure I was a goner. And nothing was done, I wasn't prepared and I would have left such a mess behind. Financially, physically with all this stuff I had, and still, I need to sift through things and clean it up.

That is one of the biggest fears that people have, the mess that now someone else has to clean up.

I hope that I still get the chance to do it before it's too late.

And there is more. Imagine, dying and you don't have a will...what will happen to all your money?

Your jewelry? Your property and your investments? Or will everyone end up fighting over it all. Make sure you have a Will!!! Or the government could end up with it.

At this time, I have been told that there is no surgical treatment available to repair or replace this mitral valve. From time to time I go on line to see if there are any new developments in my area of need with this heart. Medications do help but I still do a little work and that I am grateful for. But the symptoms are brutal. I am out of breath from walking from my bedroom to the washroom; I am out of breath from just dressing, or putting my face on and combing my hair. I am too tired to drive myself anywhere at the moment.

It could become a real family breaker. So I think I will lead by example and get started here to make it easier on my partner and my family.

If Christmas is hard,
If you've lost someone dear.
Just look in your heart,
And you'll know they're still here.

The star in the sky,
The light falling snow.
The robin outside,
It seems like they know.

If this is a time,
When you're struggling through.

Just do what you can,
For what matters, is you.

There's no need to be merry,
There's no need to bright.
Just do what you can,
It will all be alright.
-Author Unknown.

Chapter 23:

Where Do I Start?

Since you are reading this, there is still time!

Since I already have an illness that could take me out at some point, I don't know when. It could be in five years or it could be in 5 months. It would behoove me to have a Power of Attorney drawn up. And this I did. I had an old Will and POA, but really it wasn't accurate any more. So if the people have changed in your life, you got divorced, or had a baby, your executor passed away or moved out of the country, you remarried...it is time for a new Will. (You don't want your ex to get your belongings do you? It is possible if you don't change or update things.

Power of Attorney

What is the reason for this? Well you actually need at least 2...one for personal care; the other is for your property. If or when by chance you are not in a position to decide what needs to be done to look after your physical body, or your property, you need to choose someone you trust (with your life) as your Power of Attorney. Your POA (Power of Attorney) when it's needed to make decisions based on what you have written in your POA. He or she will make decisions as if it were you making the decision. By having a POA written out, you take the guilt, stress and anxiety away from your children, by directing them to follow your wishes. And if you have opted to have a DNR Do Not Resuscitate, your loved ones will not feel guilty for following your wishes.

The following are also things you may want to think about.

Prepare your Will and POA

To prepare a Will and a Power of Attorney is absolutely necessary. If doing the paperwork is too difficult for you, ask a friend or relative to help you. By not following through on these things, your wishes will absolutely not be known and it will make things so much more difficult for your family. If for some reason you can't afford to pay a lawyer to do this for you. Go on line and find the forms that are available. Fill in the spaces and have 2 witnesses sign the forms at the same time, so that you are having your signature observed by the witnesses. Make sure that the dates are the same for all three signatures. (Yours and the 2 witnesses.) Appendix 1

As I mentioned earlier, I had a birthday party and gave away some of my valued possessions. I thought it was an excellent idea. And my guests, mainly family and a couple of close friends were happy to take some of these things off my hands. It ended up that it also helped me when I had to move, it was less to pack. I also liked it that the boys discussed it nicely, no fighting or arguing about things. So it was a win/win situation for all concerned. It was also nice to know where my things went and that they appreciate it.

Give stuff away before you pass away. Now-a-days, we have so many things, that we are definitely having it too good. We don't need all that stuff. Get rid of it. Either sell it, or give it away.

Now some of us have had a choke hold on our material things. I'm guilty... And others have lost a lot, guilty there too. And as we have often hear; we can't take it with us. Having had two marriages that ended in divorce and the other one that ended in death of my husband, I have had numerous times where the possessions of the marriage were not fairly split.

I never felt good about fighting over possessions. And my ex's ended up with the better share of things. And in my last marriage, my ex arranged to have the furniture stored at his friends. And when I got situated in Lindsay he brought a trailer load of things to my place after I had requested certain things like my mother's crystal, my dining room boxes with dishes, and the legs to the dining room table. And what he brought was not what I had wanted or needed, the legs to the table never ever arrived, nor did my china cabinet. The dining room dishes were lost and the crystal disappeared. And a box of family pictures also was declared missing. So obviously if I didn't receive it, and Bill didn't because I was at his apartment and he didn't have it either, he said he didn't sell it....who knows. It was perhaps taken by his friends, because I never saw them again either. As for my wheel chair, I certainly could have used it, and actually Bill could have used it towards the end of his life, it the wheelchair also mysteriously disappeared out of a garage, from people across the street, and my pine jelly cabinet had a similar demise ...and at this point it really is just material things, it can be replaced but,...you know what they say. You can't take it with you, and obviously I couldn't. When people you trust start helping themselves to your property...they might as well have stolen it. So at some point there will be a reckoning. Karma also has something to say and do about it. All I know is I still have too much stuff! But it is getting sorted out.

Thankfulness! Be grateful for what you have. Be grateful for waking up each morning. Be grateful you have a roof over your head, food in the house, and OHIP coverage. Be grateful if you have a doctor who cares about you.   Be thankful that if you require medical intervention you don't have to wait an extraordinary length of time. Be grateful if you have a caring family and a spouse who ends up making your life easier and not more difficult.

If you are having trouble exercising thankfulness and gratefulness…buy a Journal and each day start writing what you are happy about. What makes you happy? Do you have faith? Do you have fears?

Are you afraid to die? Are you content in life? Are you able to talk to someone about your prognosis?

Is there something you would still like to accomplish? Do you have a bucket list?

Live like you are dying. If we all lived like we are dying, we would use our time better, we would accomplish more. We would be happier. We would spend time with the people we wanted to spend time with.

You see we forget to live like we are dying. And the fact is that we are all dying. Some of us are given a death sentence, but we have to remember, for the moment we are born, we have they say been given X number of years, so in essence we are all terminal. None of us are getting out alive. We are all going to die. So once you are reconciled to the fact that we are all going to die and leave the planet one day.

Dying is part of life. It is as natural as the sun rising each morning and setting each evening. We all have a place in the grand scheme of things, and we are all able to enjoy life if we allow it to happen. We are also able to enjoy the time we have left before we die.

It is sad for those who are left behind. It is sad for the one who is leaving as well. I personally think that I feel like I am going to be missing things. Like for instance the weddings of my grandchildren. The trips, or visit to certain areas in the province and Canada. Seeing the Rocky Mountains, Jasper, and Banff, those beautiful mountains! Am I going to be here for some of these things and events?

I remember when my Dad was dying, he said to me, I will miss you so much, but I thought since he was the one that was going to be leaving us, how could he be going to miss us. I must admit, I think I didn't understand totally how he felt. I thought since I was being left behind, I would be missing him. Dad would be dying. I was too insensitive I think. Yes of course, I was. In 2002, I thought differently than I do now.

It is difficult to imagine how a dying person would feel, since we have never been in that position before. All I can say is that at the moment, I do know a bit about how Dad must have felt. Because I do believe I am feeling similar emotions at the moment. My heart is not working well! Last week I also found out that I have to have a 5 cm polyp surgically removed. The doctor who found it said it was too large to remove at the time of the colonoscopy. We spoke about it afterwards, and decided that I would have it surgically removed. He said it looked ok, not cancerous, but he also said if left it will become cancerous. So while I am waiting, I hope it stays the same and does not change. I do have a family history with colon cancer, my brother Peter Spaans had his colon removed and was on a colostomy since 2004 and in 2016 was diagnosed with pancreatic cancer. So I need to be proactive concerning my health.

The thing is...I now feel like I will be missing people. I will miss Lorne, my sons, their families, my friends, my church, my art, my writing. And I also feel sad that I will be causing them pain by leaving them behind. But it can't be avoided.

Live with Forgiveness: Has someone been nasty to you? Have they hurt you? Taken something from you? Forgive them. The fact that they have hurt you and you have let it slide is not necessarily a good thing for the friend or child, brother or sister. By forgiving them you make them feel better but the one who is going to feel best of all is You. Forgiveness is a gift you give to yourself. After you have forgiven someone in your own heart, they will treat you better. There is no more wondering, when is she going to lash out at me? You are able to go forwards and live together as if nothing had every happened. One needs to keep moving forward, not backwards. Life is meant to be lived not wasted with fear or anger.

Regrets Resolve Them: if due to unforeseen circumstances you have annoyed, or hurt someone, do something to resolve it. Go for contentment. We should all live with contentment.

Live in Peace: When someone passes away, we often say, or write, RIP so and so. So why can't we *live in peace*?

Let your last year or months be peaceful and content. For that matter, why do we only do that for the last months of our life? Why not every day? Why not for everyone? I know that I resolve to be happy until I stop breathing. When this ticker decides to tic no more, I will have done my best to make myself happy.

It is a choice after all. We can make good choices every day.

Birthday Party - Christmas in July:

Since we live in the country on the edge of a rocky bush...we need to be prepared for everything and anything.

In the winter we have snow moving equipment available to clean out the yard. Man you need it up here. We have seen the municipal snow grader who does some of the cleaning of the wintery roads gets stuck. When he reached the crest of the hill, he couldn't go forward. Well before we knew it he had slid down the hill and into the ditch. After a long period of 30-45 minutes the grader inched his way out using his blade to pull himself back onto the road. It was brilliant to watch!

Winter can and is beautiful here in Dunchurch. As you drive through the village, Whitestone Lake is on both sided of

Highway 124 which leads from Sundridge to Parry Sound. You actually can go from the north to south or south to north part of the lake, with a small boat. There are rocks right beside the channel.

The trees laden with snow are a sight for sure, right out of a Christmas card. But, unfortunately the weather can get overwhelming and if you don't have 4 wheel drive…driving sucks and you may not even get in to see us…So we are going to start a new tradition. Christmas in July!…. The traffic is better, no snow to worry about. We'll go swimming instead of ice fishing. A nice bonfire in the evening, we'll roast marshmallow when it's safe to have an open fire! We will sing campfire songs, and Christmas Carols if you are up for Christmas in July! Awe such fun. Building memories together! It will be very special.

The above thoughts are all things to tell your children (when you have them) about your Oma Cat and Lorne who lived in the cottage country up north of Maple Island in Dunchurch.

The Bucket List: These are things that you saved to do last...like going to a special town in another province or state. Give something to someone special. Jump out of an airplane. Zip line through the tree tops. Do something outrageous. I may not personally do that, but I know that my friends have done things like jump out of a plane...

My friend Trish always wanted a turquoise convertible... and she did buy one. She loved it and when people would stop to admire her Marino Convertible, she would tell them, it was on her bucket list.

Writing Letters to Loved Ones: This is a very good idea to write a letter to a brother or sister...Mom and Dad if they are still alive. Also write to your children and grandchildren; plan a letter that expresses your love, what you're feeling and what you think. A letter such as this will be kept by your family forever. You can tell them your favourite story about them. What you are remembering…how you had such a good time with ….. Don't send them all the same letter. Make it personal. I wish I had a letter from my Grandmother.

You can sometimes write what you can't freely say to the person without crying or being emotional. It is important to write your peace and express your love. Give some examples of 'love' in your family. I would make sure my family gets these letters while I am still alive. Then there is still an opportunity to talk about what you had written.

Arrange for anything that must be done after you pass away: You may have gone to a lawyer or your executor, to go over things that need doing...While there you would probably have done a new Will and Power of Attorneys.

Get rid of things: Place everything you are cleaning up, in a few piles... things that will be distributed to family and friends, other things to be given to charity and lastly, things that need to go to the dump!

You have made the arrangements for the funeral of your loved one. When they die...

Make sure you let the funeral home know where to pick up the body. Write or complete the obituary. Pick out clothes for the deceased to be buried in/ or cremated in.

Death Certificates: Make sure you receive at least 10 death certificates. It seems like every one after death needs for you to prove the family member is truly dead...so there is another certificate.

(Insurance company, deed to residence or property or both. Cottage deed. Final Tax needs certificate. Service and Utilities, tax, hydro, water, cable, & credit cards etc. They want you to prove that the one who normally pays the bills has actually died.)

In Canada, Death Benefit: There is also a $2500.00 death benefit paid to the executor or the spouse of the deceased if you live in Canada. I haven't researched whether other countries do this as well, so if you're in USA, in Europe or some other continent; it is worth it to check it out if your country pays a death benefit.

The executor must do a final tax return for the deceased. There are other forms to fill out. There's the application of the death benefit, apply for that for sure.

Have a Theme Party, or celebrate some other event an excuse to party before the wake. Plan a special party yourself or have a relative plan a party. Perhaps a theme party. The oldest meets the youngest. A picnic party. Whatever turns your crank.

Plan where your ashes will go

….To the lake, cottage, cemetery etc. Mine are going to be spread amongst the trees at the cottage. I have also arranged for 5 trees to be planted at the cottage by my grandchildren, in memory of me. Maybe Lorne can put a bench down so that whoever is visiting can sit down and reminisce with me. I may have a stone as a marker…actually I am thinking that big boulder down the hill, and there would be room for trees to be planted as well.

If it's your thought of going home, build a nice memorial area on your property. I like a spot where you can have privacy. Place a comfy bench for sitting, bird watching, reading or just looking. A tree, planted in memory of your loved one. I know Guy St. Julien artist friend who can build you a very unique bench. Seriously!

I truly believe that the most important key to happiness, is keeping your life simple. It's when you complicate things, or over think or plan your life that's when the problems start to pile up.

We can be very happy by enjoying those around us. If you don't enjoy them, find others to fit the bill. Some people's kids just aren't that nice. They are selfish, greedy, mouthy, opinionated, and bully's. How would you like to spend your days and nights with that? Most wouldn't! So de-friend the miserable ones who don't have your best interest at heart, or make you happy.

Friendships are a two way streets. You don't have to see your best friend every day. But there is an unwritten rule, you are and will always be true to the friendship and your friend. Even if you don't see them for a year, your friend knows that you love them and care for them. And when you do get together, it is as though you had never been gone.

Chapter 24:

Got Your Affairs in Order?

If you don't have a Will yet, do so especially if you have changed your marital status, have added children to your family, bought a house, or if you travel a lot, if you are ill, you've come into money, won the lottery, retired etc. you need to make a NEW Will.

For People who are scheduled for surgery it is a good idea to be prepared, especially if you are older, and have children.

Your children love you and don't want you to suffer. If you have by now brought up the subject of your passing away, they may be encouraged now to talk to you about your last months on this earth.

If you are not well, and are booked to having a procedure under anesthetics, get your affairs in order as well.

For instance in 2011, I have my left hip replaced, and because I was living on my own, I didn't have someone to advocate for me, I had to make sure that my affairs were in order. In the event that I had a stroke during surgery or a heart attack that left me incapacitated, it was imperative that I prepare a Power of Attorney (POA).

Knowing that I was prepared was of comfort for me. My Power of Attorney for Health Care was done so that my children wouldn't have to make a tough decision that could leave them feeling guilty for life. You think, my son's wouldn't be upset about making a life and death decision. But oh, they would.

They did have experience with that years ago when their dad fell at a job site in Kingston, Ontario. The accident happened before 8 am in the morning, and he lay in a construction hole were the footing for the building was poured. He either had a heart attack or a stroke and fell into the hole. When the workers started to filter in, someone saw Kurth laying in the bottom of the hole, 911 was called and he was taken to Kingston General Hospital. There they determined he had broken his neck in the fall.

Kurth was put on life support, and in the mean time, the police had gone through his phone to find next of kin. Our eldest son was phoned and told the story about his dad's accident, and it was suggested that he and his brother go to Kingston to say goodbye to him.

That is what they did. Peter my youngest son came to my place and his brother Kurt met him and together they drove from Oshawa to Kingston to the hospital.

They met Kirsten, Kurth's wife and after speaking with their dad's doctor that morning, they were told that their dad was not able to survive without the ventilator, and that they should consider taking him off of it. He had no brain function, and there was no hope for survival. So together they agreed to have him taken off of the machine.

It was a very short time, before their dad passed away.

Now in this case, I'm not sure if he had a DNR, probably not. Automatically he was put on life support when he arrived by ambulance to the hospital. And they will do that so that family has the opportunity to still say goodbye.

If the circumstances had been different, someone could have brought a DNR directive to the hospital, and there would have been very little discussion about whether to take him off of life support.

It is always good to have an up to date POA. Can you imagine, a loved one having an accident at home. They are cleaning out a gutter, or fixing something on the roof. Heaven forbid they fall and have a terrible injury. Without a POA someone who is next of kin to the injured person would be asked to make a decision. Without a POA you could be asked if they could go on a ventilator to assist with breathing.

At the moment COVID patients are put on life support/ventilators, and given heavy duty sedation to keep them from moving or pulling equipment out of their mouth.

If these matters have never been discussed by your family, the ones who are left; are the ones who will make a decision about life and death. And if you don't want to be kept alive on a machine, you have to let someone know. And the best way to do that is to have a valid POA.

While you are at it, it is a good time to also prepare an updated Last Will and Testament. It is good to do it all at the same time. You really don't want your hard earned cash to go to the government.

You decide where your money and property will go to. And most people need to have these documents in place. That way, things run more smoothly.

You can be thankful to your parents if they have provided such documents. It makes living with the facts of life much easier and with less guilt. When someone is gravely ill, there is enough to think and worry about. So you can actually make it much easier for all concerned.

Chapter 25

Is the Cost Stopping You?

If you have a huge estate, with lots of stocks, investments, income property, the cost of a lawyer is not going to stop you. But if you are a young family with lots of bills, and not a lot of extra income to pay for a lawyer, go on line there are excellent free resources available on line. Check out the appendix for information and websites where you too can find exactly what you are looking for.

There are also financial planners who are able to help you out. Para- legal's that can help you fill out paper work. Or financial advisors like my friend Shirley who can assist you.

If you really don't have cash to spare for doing this, don't worry, go to the Appendix at the back of the book and look for the web address for Power of Attorney and Wills.

Service Canada and Service Ontario will have a number of sites where you can find a legal blank document, that can be filled in to suit your circumstances.

Provided they are signed and witnessed as instructed, they are legal in Canada.

If you are admitted to a hospital, give them a copy of your POA for health care. If one of your adult children are named as your POA their responsibility ends when the patient dies. Then you no longer need a power of attorney. If you are the executor of the deceased estate you will have a number of things to do to settle the estate and do the important things to finalize everything including the last and final income tax return.

Chapter 26

MAID

For someone who is suffering with a lot of pain and terrible symptoms, the patient often thinks to themselves, death cannot come fast enough. They are tired of living with the pain, the agony, and the restrictions. The symptoms are too much to deal with.

There are now situations where you can apply to MAID, Medical Assistance in Death in Canada. It is now legal in Canada to have assistance in death. In cases where the pain is too much to bear you can be assisted with a team of medical doctors who will evaluate your need for assistance in dying. For cancer patients, and for instance those with ALS, and others where the pain is so intense and life is near the end, thank God that there is something available for these patients.

My one and only younger brother Peter Spaans lived in Lindsay. I never saw him because he had distanced himself from his family. We both lived in Lindsay, and neither one of us ever knew, or saw each other during those years.

Peter chose MAID when cancer came to visit him a second time in the form of pancreatic cancer. When it was becoming too unbearable he had a choice at least, and that was a blessing for him. He went through the prescribed interviews with doctors and it was determined that he did qualify for MAID. He chose, or they chose,

June 17, 2017 for the day that he would slip away. It was Father's Day. He chose also to die with just his partner Dale present.

We his family of origin, were told about his cancer a year before his death. Two of his three grown children did in fact have a nice visit with him even though at his choice, he had left the family in 1986 when our mother died.

From what we know about cancer, pancreatic is one of the more nasty cancers. If you have a choice of any one of the cancers you certainly don't want to pick that one.

So what I want you to know is that most families have a story that they really don't want to tell, yet in the telling of the story, it has set up a freedom to go forward without worry.

When it comes to dying and funerals, there is usually a family member who can't be good that day. (Or days leading up to it.)

It happens in the best of families. It happens in rich families when there is a lot of money at stake. It happens in poor families, when someone has a hard time with grief, and isn't willing to get some counseling for it. It happens more than you can imagine.

It happens when the black sheep of the family doesn't bother to show up for 16 years to visit parents, brothers, sister, and his children, yet when he hears of a death in the family, will make the effort to show up at the funeral and possibly create havoc for the family and guests at the funeral home. That's why once in a while, the funeral home has off duty police on the premises just in case.

These folks that show up when they have been absent for years usually show up for a reason. You never know, they may have left something in the will for 'me' that is their thought.

In the olden day, and I'm thinking as much as 50 years ago, parents often used their 'Will' to hold their children hostage. Oh if you don't do whatever Dad wants you will not stay in his favour and receive. You screw up, you're out. I understand the motivation for it. But using a *Will to* make an adult child behave seems a little manipulative. When the following week the troubled child could turn his life around and pulls the parent back from being hit by a bus.

It seems like only recently in the last 10 years or so, people have lost their tolerance with others, especially those in their family. Some in the younger generation seems to be quite judgmental, and their answer to it is to not speak. It's too bad that these kids do that, because in some cases, the parents don't even know what they are being judged or punished for. C'est la vie! What comes around goes around, or what goes around comes around, either way, quite often the perpetrator gets a taste of it from his /or her own children.

Things happen at weddings and funerals. And if you think you will never have to deal with some of this insanity, I wish you well, but there are stories of anger, greed, and other issues that will rear its ugly head whenever there is jealousy, hate, money or abuse involved.

Weddings and funerals also brings out the best! Empathy, compassion, sharing memories and love are a few of the better qualities in humans. So I guess it depends what day it is.

Chapter 27

After the Funeral

I am often asked, "How long do I grieve?" Grief is different for everyone. For some, after a short period of time, they find themselves fitting back into a routine, the amount of sadness and crying is pretty well gone. For others, you only have to mention the name of the departed and they break into tears.

It is very personal how you deal with it. For most a counselor who is able to speak with you and relate to you is a good start. But you have to make sure it's a good fit.

The thing that I also want to remind you of is…that your dear spouse, mom or dad wouldn't want you to stop living, or enjoying your life. Just because you are alive and they aren't; doesn't mean that you stop living. Your loved one would want you to be laughing, playing, or being happy, and not sitting at home crying over them. It is no reflection on them if you are behaving in a well adjusted way.

The one you are missing is physically gone, but is always with you in memories, and in your heart. You can still think of them, look at photographs and speak to them from your heart.

The loss is huge, and the broken connection is painful, but the more you are able to talk about your loss and who you are missing, the better it is for you. We don't want you to stop talking about him or her. It takes a while to come to the acceptance stage in grief. Nobody expects you to achieve this overnight.

It is possible the first few times after the loss of your loved one, the moment someone mentions his name, tears well up in your eyes and you physically can't help but sob. That is understandable. And others will understand if that happens. There is no such thing as being a sissy, or immature, or embarrassing. At some point grief will find its way to everyone.

The pain of grief and sadness is the cost of love. If you hadn't loved the person so much, it wouldn't have been so painful. If you could have just not liked her that much...or if grandma hadn't been so nice to you, it would have been easier. But that isn't how it is. Grief is Real! Grief Hurts! As you go through the various steps of grief, you will come to realize that you are getting used to what they call a new normal.

When your heart is broken, it takes time to heal, so take your time. One day it will not hurt as much anymore, and a few months beyond that you will realize that the pain is bearable. You are getting used to it. You will not be as teary about it, you will still miss, but the pain is tolerable. And you are still so happy that you had this wonderful love experience in your life.

Live with Forgiveness Has someone been nasty to you? Have they hurt you? Taken something from you? Forgive them. The fact that they have hurt you and you have let it slide is not necessarily a good thing for the friend or child, brother or sister. By forgiving them you make them feel better but the one who is going to feel best of all is You. Forgiveness is a gift you give to yourself. After you have forgiven someone in your own heart you will treat each other better. There is no more wondering, when is she going to lash out at me? You are able to go forwards and live together as if nothing had every happened.

One needs to keep moving forward, not backwards. Life is meant to be lived not wasted with fear or anger.

For those who you can't forgive personally, forgive them in your heart. The effect is the same. All will be better and grateful for the act of forgiveness.

Chapter 28:

Losing a Child

The moment you find out you are pregnant in most cases you are so happy to becoming parent. The planning, the preparations and the excitement of a new baby coming to be part of your family is such a wonderful time in the life your marriage, and your family.

The day that little bundle arrives, for some is the happiest day in their lives. Some have waited much more than 9 months, some have waited and waited and is some cases, some would be mothers never get the physical opportunity to become a mother. And the pain for some is unbearable.

For those who are fortunate enough to become a mother, there is no greater joy.

This joy is part of the birth process, the pain is quickly forgotten. This joy is also part of the anticipation of adopting that chosen child.

When that baby goes home with you, you feel as if you are on top of the world. You plan to be the best parents, promise that new life to look after and love him or her with all your might. You never for a moment think that there will ever be a day that you will not be able to protect, or save or look after that little one.

As a chaplain, I have experienced the sadness of a number of parents who had their baby or toddler suddenly taken away to death.

There have also been older parents who had their adult children die to heart attack or an accident. The age of the child, does not really make any difference to the parent. A child is always a child to the parent. They're always a mother or father's child. Their baby! The age of the child does not matter at all...in the case of the married adult child, they are often leaving a spouse and children behind. The age then is immaterial, because they are still someone's child.

Losing a child they say is worse than losing a spouse. And as much as you love a spouse, the love a parent has for their child, whether it is a natural child, or an adopted child, there is no difference. The loss is overwhelming.

The price we pay for having loved someone in your life...is grief. The more you loved, the more it hurts. This is of course so true. When parents loose a child, it is grief beyond imagination. But look at it this way, the moment you look at that little bundle, your heart flips, and you are in love. Instant Love! This love does not diminish, quite the opposite, as the baby grows, it does things, and says things and actually you fall even deeper in love with this child. Should something happen and this child is taken away by death...the pain is overwhelming. To never see that face again, to not be able to cuddle and hug and kiss that sweet face, your flesh and blood...is the most unbearable thing that a parent can endure. The hurt of losing a child is so painful it is the most horrible thing that could happen to a parent.

Time does not heal. Nothing that anyone can do will make it better. This is a thing that takes many sunrises and sunsets to get accustomed too. It becomes a new normal. I have other children that I love the same way, so I have to be there for them.

Otherwise they will think I don't love them. And that isn't true of course. My children are my life. So you put one foot in front of the other and you go through the motion of healing one second at a time. And after a good long talk with yourself you promise yourself that you can do it. You cannot stop living, enjoying and laughing. It is ok to forget once in a while that you have lost a most wonderful precious child. The child wants you to continue living and being the good mother and father you were to him. And life goes on.

Unfortunately these heartaches cannot be avoided. The following pages offer you some assistance in dealing with the various situations that you may need help with.

I wish you success in getting your affairs in order. And if you are reading this, there is still time.

As a minister and chaplain I wish you all the love and healing a heart can hold. Life is not always easy. And when we lose someone very precious, we don't always see how we will ever recover. In some instances, depending who we are and what we do, and who we have around us will determine how we heal.

We can never tell a mother or a father how to heal or what is expected of a parent to heal after the loss of a child.

We can only hope that our lives will still have hope for us. It is always the hope for parents that the children outlive their parents. That is the natural order of things. It is not natural to even think that a parent should outlive their child.

"There is no foot so small that it cannot leave an imprint on this world."

Author Unknown

Appendix 1

https://www.attorneygeneral.jus.gov.on.ca/english/family/pgt/poa.pdf

The above website is from the Government of Canada, it contain, information booklet about the 2 different Power of Attorneys and also contains forms for Continuing Power of Attorney for Property and Power of Attorney for Personal Care. If you are outside of Canada...type Power of Attorney into your browser and it will bring you to your local information about POA.

For further information regarding any changes as the years pass always check the website.

www.service.canada.ca

www.service.ontario.ca

To the ever changing life or rules and regulations also consult the CRA, Canada Revenue Agency https://www.canada.ca/en/revenue-agency.html

There is also a death benefit available for those who have contributed to CPP.

Go to Service Canada, type in Death Benefit, and there is an application available.

These websites are Canadian. If you are in a different country, I am sure there is an equivalent website available.

Type: "Last Will and Testament" into your browser.

Type: "Power of Attorney" in to your browser and see what is offered in your country.

Appendix 2

In the province of Ontario, you are able to find information about a Last Will and Testament if you go to Service Ontario website.

If you are looking for Free information and a Will Kit...type

'Free Will Kit' (and your province) into your browser. There should be a variety of Sources available.

Once your Will is completed and ready to sign, make sure that when you sign your Will, your 2 witnesses are present to sign at the same time and on the same date to sign.

Appendix 3
PLANNING GUIDE WITH FAMILY FOR A FUNERAL OR MEMORIAL SERVICE

Contact Name/Executor

_____

tele:_____

PROPER GIVEN NAMES OF DECEASED:_____

_____

Lived in/at:_____

_____

Preferred to be called:

_____

Nickname of deceased:_____

Date of Birth:_____

Where Born

_____

Name of Parents:

_____

Lived here as a child:

_____
_____

Went to school:

_____
_____

High School:

_____
_____

College/ University:

_____
_____

Spouse's Name:

_____

What did couple look like on wedding day? How did they meet?

Married on:

_____

Married at:

_____

Married:_____ years

Divorced (Yes)   Remarried (N) Yes

*_____ was a Wife, Mother, Grandmother, Mother-in-law, Daughter-in-law, Aunt, Niece, Friend, Teacher...etc

*_____ was a Husband, Father, Grandfather, Father-in-law, Son-in-law, Uncle, Nephew, Friend, Teacher ...etc.

Names of Children And their Spouse (if any)

1._____
_____

2._____
_____

3._____
_____

4._____
_____

Names of Grandchildren:_____
_____
_____
_____

What did they call their parent/grandparents etc…Mom, grandma, baba, oma, etc:
_____

Other info:

Other special people that you would like to acknowledge:_____

_____
_____

Important Defining Moments in Life:

1:_____
_____

2:_____
_____

3:_____
_____

4:_____
_____

5:_____
_____

Special Dates Important to the Deceased and the family:

Hobbies and Interests:

_____
_____
_____
_____
_____

Best times that we had together:

_____
_____
_____
_____
_____

Favourite time of year:

_____
_____

Why_____

_____
_____

Favourite holiday:

_____
_____
_____

Favourite Sport to Play:

_____
_____
_____

Special Teams to support:

_____
_____
_____

Favourite Sports or shows to watch on TV:

_____
_____

Who would be participating with him or her?

_____

Like to Travel?   Yes   No.

Favourite Places to travel to:

_____
_____
_____
_____
_____

Employment information: Self Employed: Y
Name of Company

_____
_____
_____

Located:_____
_____
_____

Professional affiliations:

_____
_____
_____
_____

Political Affiliations:

_____

Church Affiliations:

_____

since_____
Membership(s):

_____
_____
_____

Special Pets:

_____
_____
_____

Special Charities:

_____
_____
_____

Stories you would like to share- Or- special times or places shared with family and friends etc. Do the children wish to share a thought about the deceased?

Yes/ No: If Yes... there is room on next page:

1.

2.

3.

4.

5.

6.

Was deceased a member of Armed Services?

_____

Where and how did they serve?

_____

_____

Legion Member Branch #_____

What caused death?

_____

At home or hospital?

_____

Name of Hospital:

_____

_____

How long in Hospital?

Was family present at time of death? Y

THOUGHTS OR PLANS FOR FUNERAL/MEMORIAL SERVICE /INTERNMENT

Date:_____

NAME OF CEMETERY:

_____

_____

Address: _____

_____

_____p.c._____

_____

TIME: _____ am/pm

Interment to follow:

Where? _____

_____

Address: _____

_____

Cremation: _____ **Other** _____

Eulogy to be ready by :

_____

Scripture reading's:

_____

_____

Inclusion of 23rd Psalm or Other:

_____

Inclusion of Lord's Prayer: Yes   No

Hail Mary: N/A   Yes

Inclusion of a special poem or reading:
_____

If yes, read by someone else?
Who:_____

Special Music
Requests:_____
_____

_____

Pall Bearers:

1.

2.

3.

4.

5.

6

Appendix 4

Medical Assistance In Dying MAID

It can be stressful for individuals to contemplate their end-of-life options. With the legalization of medical assistance in dying in June of 2016, Canadians were granted another option at the end of life, but confusion over interpreting the new law and understanding the process has led to unnecessary trauma and obstacles for people and their loved ones.

If you have questions about your personal end-of-life care options, we encourage you to contact your health care provider.

If you do not have a health care provider, please call Dying With Dignity Canada's Support team by emailing support@dyingwithdignity.ca or calling us toll-free at 1-844-395-3640. Your questions will be answered, or you will be directed to the appropriate site so as to avoid any unnecessary trauma and obstacles for patients and their loved ones.

About the Author
Rev. Catharina Bowers

Rev. Catharina Bowers is a semi retired non denominational minister who does pulpit supply at a lovely rural church in Magnetawan. She is the founder of https://Reflections101.com and runs a Facebook group with the same name.

She writes a blog every week and it is published on Sunday morning at 6AM EST. Her blogs started on August 29th 2019. There are about 100 blogs available for your reading pleasure.

Her blogs are also published in the Great North Arrow an online Newspaper out of Magnetawan, Ontario.

She is a member of Women of Whitestone.

If you would like to receive updates about blogs, please join the Reflections101.com web site by sending your email address and request to... https://Reflections101.com or email Cat@Reflections101.com

She and her husband Lorne King live in Dunchurch. She is the mother of 2 grown sons, grandmother of 5 beautiful grandchildren who call her Oma. She is an artist, writer, lyricist, sculptress and designer. Reiki Master, Author of the Cosmic Cradle, Journey into Self Discovery.

She will answer your questions on end of life preparations and spirituality.

rev.catharina.bowers@hotmail.com or Cat@Reflections101.com

Contributing Author
Rev. Michael Bishop

Rev. Michael Bishop is the former head of Spiritual Care for Lakeridge Health in Oshawa. He is a semi retired minister and hospital chaplain. Michael is the father of 3 adult children and a grandfather of 7, soon there will be 8 grandchildren to love. Michael lives in Clarington, Ontario.

Michael is the author of Life's Ultimate Adventure.

Michael celebrates a wonderful Celebration of Life in the Durham Region area. To request Michael, phone him at 289-685-6585 to confirm his availability.

Michael also writes a beautiful, thought provoking blog called Bishopsthoughts.com
https://bishopsthoughts.com

He also facilitates a grief group on line through Facebook.   Call: 289-685-6585 or email him at bishopsthoughts@mail.com

He welcomes hearing from you. As an experienced hospital chaplain of many years, Michael is open to comments and questions.

www.ingramcontent.com/pod-product-compliance
Lightning Source LLC
Chambersburg PA
CBHW060824220526
45466CB00003B/968